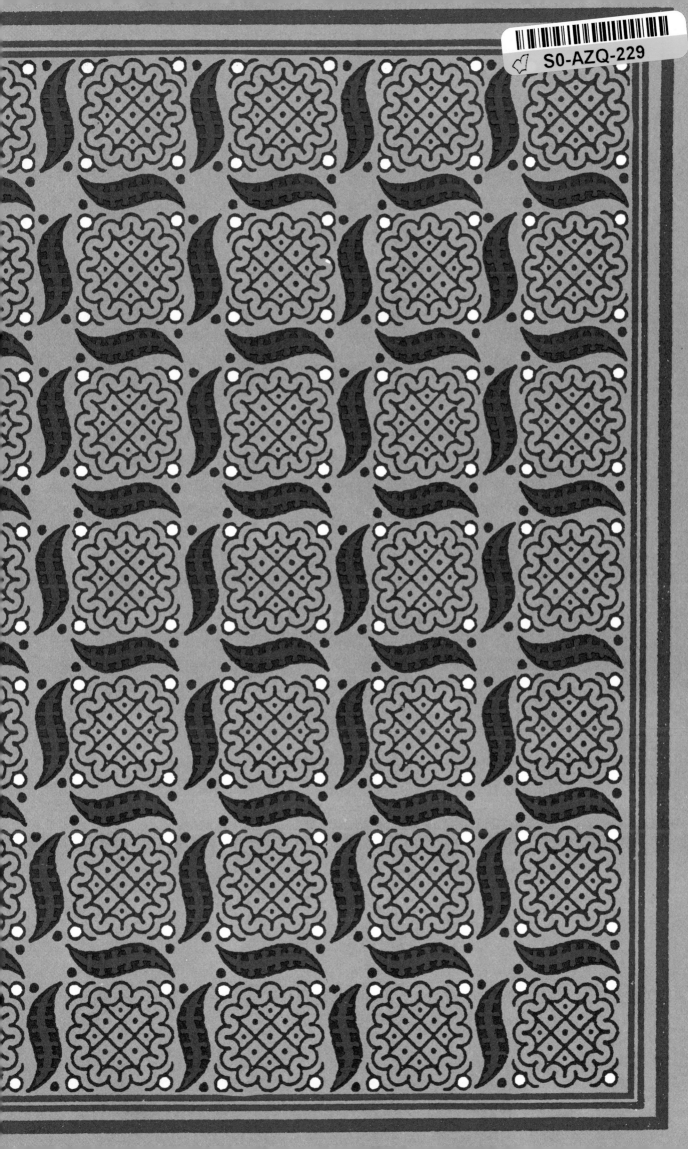

THE ART OF THE BOOK

THE
ART
OF
THE
BOOK

CHARLES HOLME

Dorset Press
New York

Originally published 1914 by
The Studio Limited
London, Paris, New York

This edition published 1990 by Dorset Press
a division of Marboro Corporation

Copyright this edition © Studio Editions Ltd., London 1990

Printed and bound in GDR

ISBN 0-88029-504-X

LIST OF ARTICLES

PREFATORY NOTE

THE Editor desires to express his thanks to the following who have kindly assisted in the preparation of this volume :—to the Trustees of the Kelmscott Press for permission to reproduce the pages printed in the three types designed by William Morris, and to Mr. Emery Walker for the valuable assistance he has rendered in the reproductions of these particular pages, and also the page of Proctor's Greek type; to Mr. Lucien Pissarro for allowing the three pages by the Eragny Press to appear; to Mr. C. H. St. John Hornby, whose page by the Ashendene Press has been especially set up for this volume; to Mr. Philip Lee Warner for permission to show two pages by the Riccardi Press; to Messrs. Chatto & Windus for the page by the Florence Press; to Messrs. Methuen & Co. for the page printed in the " Ewell " type; to Messrs. H. W. Caslon & Co. for the page of their new " Kennerley " type; to Messrs. P. M. Shanks & Sons for the page of " Dolphin Old Style " type; to Mr. F. V. Burridge for the two pages especially set up at the London County Council Central School of Arts and Crafts; to Messrs. George Allen & Co. for permission to reproduce the two pages designed by Mr. Walter Crane; to Mr. Percy J. Smith for the book-opening designed by him; to the Cuala Press, the Vincent Press, the Reigate Press, Messrs. B. T. Batsford, Messrs. J. M. Dent & Sons, Messrs. George Routledge & Sons, Messrs. Siegle, Hill & Co., for permission to show various pages from their publications; and to Mr. J. Walter West, R.W.S., for the pages designed by him. ❧ The Editor's thanks are due to the various bookbinders whose work has been lent for illustration, and to Monsieur Emile Lévy for the loan of the photographs of Mr. Douglas Cockerell's bindings; to Mr. John Lane for permission to illustrate the cover designs by Aubrey Beardsley; and to Messrs. George Newnes for the end-paper design by Mr. Granville Fell. ❧ The Editor is also indebted to the various Continental and American publishers, printers, type-founders, bookbinders and book-decorators who have kindly placed at his disposal the examples of their work shown in the foreign sections; particularly to Herren Gebrüder Klingspor, the Bauersche Giesserei, Herr Emil Gursch, Herr D. Stempel, Herren Genzsch and Heyse, MM. G. Peignot et fils, Monsieur L. Pichon, and Monsieur Jules Meynial for the pages of type especially set up for this volume.

GREAT BRITAIN

BRITISH TYPES FOR PRINTING BOOKS. BY BERNARD H. NEWDIGATE

TO judge rightly of the good or bad features of types used for printing books, we should have some acquaintance at least with the earlier forms from which our modern types have come. Let us therefore glance at the history of the letter from which English books are printed to-day. ✠ The earliest printed books, such as the Mainz Bible and Psalters, were printed in Gothic letter, which in its general character copied the book-hands used by the scribes in Germany, where these books were printed. In Italy, on the other hand, the Gothic hand did not satisfy the fastidious taste of the scholars of the Renaissance, who had adopted for their own a handwriting of which the majuscule letters were inspired, or at least influenced, by the letter used in classical Rome, of which so many admirable examples had survived in the old monumental inscriptions. For the small letters they went back to the fine hand which by the eleventh and twelfth centuries had gradually been formed out of the Caroline minuscules of the ninth and had become the standard book-hand of the greater part of Latin Europe. When the Germans Sweynheim and Pannartz brought printing into Italy, they first printed books in a very beautiful but somewhat heavy Roman letter of strong Gothic tendency. It seems, indeed, to have been somewhat too Gothic for the refined humanistic taste of that day; and when they moved their press to Rome, it was discarded in favour of a letter more like the fashionable scrittura umanistica of the Renaissance. Other Italian printers had founts both of Gothic and of Roman types. The great Venetian printer Jenson, for instance, and many of his fellows printed books in both characters; but the Roman gradually prevailed, first in Italy, then in Spain and France, and later on in England. In Germany, on the other hand, the cradle-land of the craft, Gothic letter of a sadly debased type has held its own down to this day. Even in Germany, however, the use of Roman type has gained ground of late years, nationalist feeling notwithstanding. ✠ The Roman type used by the early Italian printers is, then, the prototype from which all other Roman founts are descended. Its development may be traced through such Roman type as was used by Aldus at Venice, by Froben at Basle, by the Estiennes in Paris, by Berthelet and Day in London, by Plantin at Antwerp, by the Elzevirs at Leyden and Amsterdam, and by printers generally right through the seventeenth century and the greater part of the eighteenth. Through all these years types still kept what modern printers call their " old-face " character, which they had acquired from the scrittura umanistica of the Italian Renaissance. In the seventeenth century the letters of the Roman alphabet began to acquire certain new features at the hands of the copper-plate engravers, who supplied the book illustrations of the period. Working with the burin instead of the pen, they naturally used a sharper and finer line and also modified somewhat the curves of the letters, which tended to become more stilted and less open. The tail of the " R," for instance, which in Jenson's type is thrust forward at an angle of about forty-five degrees, at the hands of some of the seventeenth-century engravers tends to drop more vertically, as in the " R " of " modern " type, the development of which we are seeking to trace. How far and how soon the lettering of the engravers of illustrations came to modify the letters cast by the type-founders is a question which invites further research. A material piece of evidence is supplied by the " Horace " printed by John Pine in 1733. Instead of being printed from type, the text of this book, together with the ornaments and illustrations, was printed from engraved copperplates. In date it was some sixty years prior to the earliest books printed in " modern-faced " type in this country; yet in the cut of the lines and the actual shape of the letters many distinguishing features of the " modern " face may already be traced. What these features became may be seen best by comparing an alphabet of the " old " with one of the " modern " face printed below it :

ABCDEFGHIJKLMNOPQRSTUV

ABCDEFGHIJKLMNOPQRSTUV

WXYZ   1234567890

WXYZ   1234567890

abcdefghijklmnopqrstuvwxyz

abcdefghijklmnopqrstuvwxyz

The " modern " tendency may be seen in certain features of the types designed by Baskerville, who printed his first book in 1757; but it is not nearly so pronounced as in Pine's "Horace," engraved twenty-four years earlier. Baskerville's editions had an enormous vogue, not only in this country but on the Continent also, where they had considerable influence on the style of printing which then prevailed. Amongst those who felt this influence was Giambattista Bodoni, a scholar and printer of Parma, which city has lately kept the centenary of his death. To Bodoni more than anyone else the so-called " modern-face " is due. He cast a large number of founts, narrow in the " set " or width of the letters as com-

12

pared with their height, and having the excessively fine lines and the close loops and curves which are characteristic of that face. Like Baskerville he printed his books with very great care on a spacious page in large and heavily-leaded type; and although an occasional protest was raised against the ugliness of his letter, his books caught the taste of his day, and his type was copied by all the English type-founders of the time. The new fashion completely drove out the older tradition, which dated from the very invention of printing; and from the closing years of the eighteenth to the middle of the ninteenth century books were printed almost exclusively in "modern-faced" type. ℳ The older and more authentic letter had its revenge in 1843, when the publisher, William Pickering, arranged with his friend Charles Whittingham, the printer, to produce a handsome edition of Juvenal as a "leaving-present" for Eton ; and the book was to be printed from the discarded type first cut by William Caslon about the year 1724. Prior to that time English printers had gone to ·Holland for most of their type ; but Caslon's types surpassed in beauty any hitherto used in England, and the best English printing had been done from them till near the end of the century, when they were driven out by the "modern" face. Before the Juvenal was issued, a romance entitled "The Diary of Lady Willoughby," dealing with the period of the Civil Wars, was also printed in old-faced type cast from William Caslon's matrices, so as to impart to the book a flavour of the period at which the diarist was supposed to be writing. It was the day of Pugin and of the Gothic revival; and the public taste was won by the appearance of this book, printed in old-fashioned guise in the selfsame type which had been cast aside half a century before. Type-founders are generally quick to follow one another's lead in new fashions ; and before long every type-founder in England had cut punches and cast letter in that modified form of Caslon's old-faced type which printers call "old-style." Mr. Adeney of the Reigate Press has used an "old-style" fount in the extract from Camden's "Britannia" reproduced on a very small scale on page 57. The "old-style" character and the points in which it is either like or unlike the more authentic old-faced letter may be seen by comparing the two. The lower of these founts is the "old-style":

ABCDEFGHIJKLMNOPQRSTUV
ABCDEFGHIJKLMNOPQRSTUV
WXYZ   1234567890
WXYZ   1234567890

abcdefghijklmnopqrstuvwxyz

abcdefghijklmnopqrstuvwxyz

The favour which the revived "old-face" and the new "old-style" letter won for themselves in the middle of last century has suffered no diminution since. The ugly "modern-face," which we owe to Bodoni, is still used almost exclusively for certain classes of work and alternatively for others ; so that the printer is bound to be familiar with all three. For book-printing at the present day the "old style" and the "old-face" are used much more than the modern. ❧ During the fifty years that followed the revived use of Caslon's types by the Whittinghams there is little else to record about the designs of the types used for printing books, until about the year 1890, when William Morris set himself to design type, fired thereto by a lecture, given by Mr. Emery Walker, on the work of the Early Printers, to which he had listened. In the "Note by William Morris on his aims in founding the Kelmscott Press," printed after his death, he writes of the purpose which led him to print books, and of the character he sought to give his letter : "I began printing books with the hope of producing some which would have a definite claim to beauty, while at the same time they should be easy to read and should not dazzle the eye by eccentricity of form in the letters. I have always been a great admirer of the calligraphy of the Middle Ages and of the earlier printing which took its place. As to the fifteenth-century books, I had noticed that they were always beautiful by force of the mere typography, even without the added ornament with which many of them are so lavishly supplied. And it was the essence of my undertaking to produce books which it would be a pleasure to look upon as pieces of printing and arrangement of type. . . . Next as to type. By instinct rather than by conscious thinking it over, I began by getting myself a fount of Roman type. And here what I wanted was letter pure in form ; severe without needless excrescences ; solid without the thickening and thinning of the line, which is the essential fault of the ordinary modern type and which makes it difficult to read ; and not compressed laterally, as all later type has grown to be owing to commercial exigencies. There was only one source from which to take examples of this perfected Roman type, to wit, the works of the great Venetian printers of the fifteenth century, of whom Nicholas Jenson produced the completest and most Roman characters from 1470 to 1476. This type I studied with much care, getting it photographed to a big scale, and drawing it over many times before I began designing my own letter ; so that, though I think I mastered the

14

essence of it, I did not copy it servilely ; in fact, my Roman type, especially in the lower case, tends rather more to the Gothic than does Jenson's. After a while I felt I must have a Gothic as well as a Roman fount ; and herein the task I set myself was to redeem the Gothic character from the charge of unreadableness which is commonly brought against it. And I felt that this charge could not be reasonably brought against the types of the first two decades of printing : that Schoeffer at Mainz, Mentelin at Strassburg, and Günther Zainer at Augsburg, avoided the spiky ends and undue compression which lay some of the later types open to the above charge. . . . Keeping my end steadily in view, I designed a black-letter type which I think I may claim to be as readable as a Roman one, and to say the truth I prefer it to the Roman. This type is of the size called Great Primer (the Roman type is of ' English ' size) ; but later on I was driven by the necessities of the Chaucer (a double-columned book) to get a similar Gothic fount of Pica size." ❦ Pages printed in each of Morris's three founts of type are reproduced here on pages 22, 23, 33 and 34. It is interesting to compare Morris's "Golden" type—so he called his Roman fount after the "Golden Legend," which he printed from it—with the Roman letter of the Italian printers, which he studied with so much care before he began to design his type. The "Golden" type is much heavier in face than, say, that of Jenson ; and it certainly lacks the suppleness and grace of the Italian types generally. As a point of detail we may notice especially the brick-bat serifs used on Morris's capital "M" and "N," giving a certain clumsiness to these letters. The two Gothic letter founts which Morris designed, on the other hand, must be regarded as amongst the most beautiful ever cast. William Morris's types should be judged on the setting of richly decorated borders which he designed for his pages. Adding to these the designs of Sir Edward Burne-Jones, engraved on wood by W. H. Hooper, we have in the Kelmscott "Chaucer" the most splendid book which has ever been printed. ❦ The "Golden" type of the Kelmscott Press was copied freely in America and sent back to the country of its birth under several different names. In somewhat debased forms it had a vogue for a time as a "jobbing" fount amongst printers who knew little or nothing of the Kelmscott Press ; but the heaviness of its line and also its departure from accepted forms kept it from coming into general use for printing books. The interest awakened by the books printed by William Morris at Hammersmith tempted many more to set up private presses or to design private founts of type when the work of the Kelmscott Press came to an end after Morris's death, which took place in 1896. Most of such founts and the best of them followed more or less closely the letter of the early Italian printers, which, as we have seen, are the prototypes of our book letter of to-day. Even before the founding

15

of the Kelmscott Press Mr. Charles Ricketts had designed books, using some of the "old style" faces which were in general use. When the Kelmscott Press books appeared, he too was won over by what he called the "golden sunny pages" of the early Italian printers, and designed for himself the "Vale" type. In weight and general appearance it bears considerable likeness to Morris's "Golden" type, and in some ways is an improvement on it. Mr. Ricketts afterwards had the same letter cast in a smaller size for his edition of Shakespeare, whence its name of the "Avon" type. He also designed another letter, the interest of which lies in certain experiments towards the reform of the alphabet which it embodies. In the "King's" type, as Mr. Ricketts called it, many of the minuscule letters, such as e, g, t, are replaced by small majuscules. Such a departure from traditional use is too violent to give pleasure, and only two or three books were printed in this letter. The three Vale Press founts and also the punches and matrices were destroyed when the Press ceased publishing. ❧ Mr. T. J. Cobden-Sanderson and Mr. Emery Walker set up the Doves Press at Hammersmith in 1900, and designed and got cast for themselves a fount of type which follows Jenson's Roman type very closely. It differs from it chiefly in the greater regularity of its lines, and also in the squareness and brick-bat shape of some of the serifs, which are, however, less conspicuous than in Morris's "Golden" type. The Doves Press books, unlike those of the Kelmscott Press, are entirely free from ornament or decoration, and owe their remarkable beauty to what Morris styled the architectural goodness of the pages and also to the fine versal and initial letters done by Mr. Edward Johnston and Mr. Graily Hewitt. Later on we shall have something more to say about the work of these men and their school. ❧ The type of the Ashendene Press (p. 35) is modelled from that in which Sweynheim and Pannartz printed books at Subiaco, and which, as we have seen, they replaced by a purer Roman letter more in accord with the humanistic taste of their day. Morris himself designed, but never carried out, a fount of letter after the same fine model. It is a Roman type, with many Gothic features. The folio "Dante," the "Morte Darthur," the Virgil and the other books which Mr. St. John Hornby has printed from it in black and red, with occasional blue and gold, are superb examples of typography. ❧ Mr. Lucien Pissarro's little octavos have a certain personal charm of their own distinct from anything that is found in the more weighty volumes which have issued from the other private presses. The first books which he produced at his Eragny Press were printed from the Vale type belonging to his friend Mr. Ricketts. In 1903 he began printing from the "Brook" type (pp. 36 to 38), which he had designed. Although in this article we are concerned chiefly with his types, it is impossible to withhold a tribute of praise for the graceful beauty of

16

these little books, which they owe even more to the admirable way in which their different elements have been combined—type, wood-engraving, colour, printing and binding, all of them the work of Mr. and Mrs. Pissarro themselves—than to the individual excellence of any one of them. ✠ Mr. C. R. Ashbee's "Endeavour" type was designed by him for use at the Essex House Press, which he first established at Upton in the eastern suburbs of London and afterwards removed to Chipping Campden in Gloucestershire. It owes nothing to the types of the early printers, and taken by itself is not pleasing ; but it makes a very handsome page when printed in red and black, as in the Campden Song Book. The type was also cut in large size for King Edward's Prayer Book, one of the most ambitious ventures of any private press. ✠ Mr. Herbert P. Horne has designed three founts, all of them inspired by the Roman letter of the early Italian printers. The "Montallegro" type (p. 273), the first in order of date, was designed for Messrs. Updike and Co., of the Merrymount Press, Boston, and hardly falls within the scope of this article. In 1907 he designed for Messrs. Chatto and Windus a fount called the "Florence" type (p. 39), from which editions of "The Romaunt of the Rose," "The Little Flowers of St. Francis," A. C. Swinburne's "Songs before Sunrise," R. L. Stevenson's "Virginibus Puerisque" and also his Poems have been printed at the Arden Press on behalf of the publishers. It is a letter of a clean, light face, and in many ways might serve as a model for a book type for general use. The capital letters used in continuous lines, as Aldus and other great Venetians delighted to use them, are especially charming. Mr. Horne's Riccardi Press type (pp. 27 and 29) was designed for the Medici Society, and many fine editions, amongst them a Horace, Malory's "Morte Darthur," and "The Canterbury Tales," have been printed from it. It is a little heavier in face than its predecessor, the "Florence," and is a little further removed from the humanistic character. The type has also been cast successfully in a smaller size. ✠ To the number of privately owned founts of type we must add the "Ewell" (p. 31), designed by Mr. Douglas Cockerell for Messrs. Methuen and Co., who will shortly publish the first book to be printed from it, an edition of the "Imitatio Christi." It is a heavy but very graceful letter, based on one used by the Roman printer Da Lignamine. ✠ One of the most interesting of the privately owned founts is the "Otter" Greek type designed by the late Mr. Robert Proctor, and shown in the page from the Odyssey printed on page 51. The Greek letter from which most of our school classics are printed is a descendant of the cursive type introduced by Aldus at the beginning of the sixteenth century, and has the merit neither of beauty nor of clearness. The majuscules are especially ugly, being nearly always of the "modern" type which we owe to Bodoni. Proctor took as his model the finest of the old Greek founts, which was that used in the Complutensian Polyglot printed in 1514. ✠ Amongst the types sold by the founders for general use none have enjoyed such successive favour as Caslon's " Old-Face " in its various sizes ; and it is a splendid tribute to the excellence of this letter that at this day, nearly two centuries since it was first cut, it is being used more than any other face of type for printing fine books.   This Special Number of THE STUDIO is printed from Caslon's " Old-Face " type, as well as the pages, set up at the Central School of Arts and Crafts, which are shown on pages 41 and 53. The fame of Caslon's letter brought other rivals into the field besides Baskerville. One of these was Joseph Fry, a Bristol physician, who took to letter-founding in the year 1764, and cut a series of type somewhat like Baskerville's. A few years later, however, the Caslon character seems again to have recovered its old ascendancy, and Fry put on the market a new series in acknow-ledged imitation of Caslon's. Both these series of Fry's have been reissued within the last few years by Messrs. Stephenson and Blake, of Sheffield, who, in 1906, bought the type-founding business of Sir Charles Reed and Son, to whom Fry's business had eventually come. Like the revived Caslon " Old-Face " in 1843, these founts were cast from the old matrices, or from matrices struck from the old punches, so far as these had survived. ✠ Since the " old-style " founts were designed about the middle of last century, what new book types have been cast by the founders for use by the printing trade generally have as a rule been mere variations of letter already in vogue. The founders have drawn but little on the wealth of beautiful book types which in the early printed books of Italy are offered to anyone who has the good taste and the skill to adapt them to modern needs. Messrs. Shanks and Sons, the type-founders of Red Lion Square, have, however, gone to this source for their " Dolphin " series (p. 40), which has many features of beauty to com-mend it. It is based on Jenson's Roman letter, somewhat thickened in the line. The punches were cut by Mr. E. P. Prince, who also cut the Kelmscott type and many others of the private founts. ✠ Intelligent study of Italian models also gives us the " Kennerley " type (p. 49), designed by the American Mr. Goudy, which Messrs. Caslon will shortly put on the English market. This type is not in any sense a copy of early letter—it is original ; but Mr. Goudy has studied type design to such good pur-pose that he has been able to restore to the Roman alphabet much of that lost humanistic character which the first Italian printers inherited from their predecessors, the scribes of the early Renaissance. Besides being beautiful in detail his type is beautiful in the mass ; and the letters when set into words seem to lock into one another with a closeness which is common in the letter of early printers, but is rare in modern type. The

18

"Kennerley" type is quite clear to read and has few features which by their strangeness are likely to waken the prejudice of the modern reader. Since the first Caslon began casting type about the year 1724, no such excellent letter has been put within reach of English printers. ❦ So large is the proportion of books which are now set in type by machinery that, however much our sympathies may make us prefer the hand-set book, we cannot but be concerned for the characters used in machine composition. Type set by machinery generally seems to be inferior in design to that set by hand; but the inferiority is in the main accidental, and is probably due to a lesser degree of technical skill shown either in the designing or in the process of punch-cutting, which is itself done by machinery. One or two admirable faces of type have, however, been produced by the Lanston Monotype Company for setting by the monotype machine. One of these is the "Imprint" type, adapted from one of the founts used by Christopher Plantin, the famous printer of Antwerp, in the late sixteenth century. The letters are bold and clear, and pages set in them are both pleasant to look at and easy to read. At the same time the type is sufficiently modern in character not to offend by any features unfamiliar to the ordinary reader. ❦ No art can live by merely reviving and reproducing past forms, and in reviewing the share taken by the type-founders of the past and of the present in the art of the book one cannot help considering by what means and from what quarter good types are to be designed and cut in the future. We have seen that the early printers took their inspiration from the best of the contemporary book-hands. The invention of printing, however, killed the art of the scribe, and with it perished the source whence during the ages past life and beauty had been given to the letters of the alphabet and to the pages in which they were gathered. Henceforth the letters were cast in lead, and there was no influence save the force of tradition to make or keep them beautiful. Whatever change they underwent was for the worse, unless indeed it was a mere reversion to forms or features which for a while had been abandoned. ❦ Conscious of this downward tendency, which he seems to look upon as inevitable and irresistible, Mr. Guthrie, of the Pear-tree Press at Bognor, has renounced type altogether, and now prints books, like William Blake, from etched plates inscribed with his own fine book-hand. Such a method is, of course, not practicable for the vast majority of books, even if we were willing to forgo the many fine qualities which are presented in a well-printed book. Neither is any such counsel of despair warranted, for of late years the art of the scribe itself has been renewed; and most readers of THE STUDIO know something of the fine work done by the school of calligraphy established some ten years since by Mr. Edward Johnston, and still carried on by his pupil Mr. Graily Hewitt at the Central School

19

of Arts and Crafts in Southampton Row, London. May not the printer look to that school as the source whence the type-designer and type-founder shall learn to design and cut beautiful letter for his books? Not indeed that type-letter should be a mere reproduction of any written hand; rather must it bear nakedly and shamelessly all the qualities which the steel of the punch-cutter and the metal from which it is cast impose upon it. It must be easy to read as well as fair to look on, and besides carrying on the traditions of the past must respect the prejudices of the present. But only a calligrapher whose eye and hand have been trained to produce fine letter for the special needs of the printed book can have knowledge of the manifold subtleties of such letter and power to provide for them in the casting of types. If the writing schools can turn out such men, they will deserve well of all those who are interested in the art of the book. That our hope need not be vain is shown by the fact that calligraphers trained in the methods of the school have gone to Germany, and have there profoundly influenced the production of modern types; and the supreme irony of it all is that German type-founders are sending to England new types which draw their inspiration from a London school of which the English and Scottish type-founders seem never even to have heard.

Note—In the course of the preceding article the writer has had occasion to refer frequently to the type of Nicholas Jenson in its relation to the modern British founts. The Editor has therefore included amongst the examples shown a page from the "Pliny," printed by Jenson in 1476, for purposes of comparison and reference. It will be found on page 25.

Hath in the Ram his halfe cours yronne,
And smale foweles maken melodye,
That slepen al the nyght with open eye,
So priketh hem nature in hir corages;
Thanne longen folk to goon on pilgrimages,
And palmeres for to seken straunge strondes,
To ferne halwes, kowthe in sondry londes;
And specially, from every shires ende
Of Engelond, to Caunterbury they wende,
The hooly blisful martir for to seke,
That hem hath holpen whan that they were
seeke.

Bifil that in that seson on a day,
In Southwerk at the Tabard as
I lay,
Redy to wenden on my pilgrym-
age
To Caunterbury with ful devout
corage,
At nyght were come into that hostelrye
Wel nyne and twenty in a compaignye,
Of sondry folk, by aventure yfalle
In felaweshipe, and pilgrimes were they alle,
That toward Caunterbury wolden ryde.

Whan that Aprille with his shoures soote
The droghte of March hath perced to the roote,
And bathed every veyne in swich licour,
Of which vertu engendred is the flour;
Whan Zephirus eek with his swete breeth
Inspired hath in every holt and heeth

KELMSCOTT PRESS : PAGE FROM "THE WORKS OF GEOFFREY CHAUCER" PRINTED IN THE "CHAUCER" TYPE DESIGNED BY
WILLIAM MORRIS.   ILLUSTRATION BY SIR EDWARD BURNE-JONES, BART., BORDER AND INITIAL LETTER BY WILLIAM MORRIS

oua hanno penne:o fquame:o corteccia:o gufcio: come fono la Teftugine:oueramen
te hāno lapelle pulita:come fono leferpi. Taglādo laparte difopra delle péne nõ crefco
no:fueglendole rimettono:Glinfecti hanno ale di pannicoli & cofi le rondini marine
& epipiftrelli:Ma lale diquefti hanno ledita.Dalla groffa pelle efcono epeli afperi. Le
femine glhāno piu fottili.Ecauagli nel collo & eleoni nelle fpalle glhanno maggiori.
Etaffi glhanno nelle gote drento & ne piedi:lequali due cofe Trogo attribuifce ancho
ra alla lepre:& con quefto exemplo conclude che glhuomini libidinofi fono pilofi.La
lepre e uelociffima fopra tutti glanimali.Solo lhuomo mette epeli nelleta apta agene
rare:Ilche fenon e:dimoftra fterilita cofi nel mafchio come nella femina.Epeli nel hu
omo parte fingenerano infieme:parte poi. Quegli che fono infieme con lui generati
non manchono dipoi come ne anchora molto.Sonfi trouate alchune che quando get
tono ecapelli diuentano inualide:come anchora nel fluxo del meftruo. Equadrupedi
mudano ogni anno.Amafchi crefcono affai nel capo & poi nella barba. Taglati non
rimettono in fu lataglatura come rimettono lherbe:ma efcon infuori dallaradice.Cre
fcono in certe malattie & maxime nella toffa & nella uecchiaia & ne corpi morti. E cõ
géniti caggiono piu tofto a libidinofi:Ma enati crefcono piu tofto. Nequadrupedi in
groffano per la uecchiaia & lelane diuentano piu rade.Edoffi dequadrupedi fono pilo
fi: euentri fanza pelo.De chuoi de buoi cocendogli fifa optima colla.Item de tori. So
lo ditutti glanimali lhuomo mafchio ha lepoppe:neglaltri animali emafchi hāno cer
ti.fegni dipoppe:Ma ne anchora le femine hanno lepoppe fenon quelle che poffono
nutrire efigliuoli.Quegli che generano huoua non hanno poppe:Neffuno animale
ha lacte fenon quegli che generono animali.Tra gluccelli folo elpipiftrello.Credo che
fia fauolofo quello che fidice delle Streghe che mūghino ellacte inboccha a fáciulli.E
nelle Beftemie antiche quefto nome di ftreghe:Ma non fifa che uccello fi fia.

NATVRA.DELLE POPPE DEGLANIMALI.CAP.XL.

a   Lafine dolgono lepoppe dopo elparto:Ilperche Ifuezano lafinino elfexto me
         fe:conciofia che lecaualle dieno lapoppa un anno. Tutti glanimali che hāno un
ghia dun pezo non generano piu che due per uolta:ne hanno piu che due poppe & q̄l
le nel pectignone:nel medefimo luogho lhanno quelle che hanno lunghia didue pezi
& fono cornute:le uacche quattro:le pecore & capre due.Quelle che partorifcono piu
chc due & hanno le dita nepiedi hanno molte poppe per tutto eluentre in due filari.
Le troie generofe hanno dodici poppe:le uulgari due meno.Similmente le cagne.Al
chune hanno quattro in mezo del corpo:come fono lepanthere.Alchune due chome
fono le lioneffe.Lohelephante folo ha due poppe fotto lebraccia & nõ nelpecto.Nef
funa che habia dita nepiedi ha poppe nel pectigione.Eporcellini prima nati fucciano
leprime poppe & benche habbino laltre preffo alla bocca:ciafchuno conofce lefue in
quello ordine che e nato & cõ quella finutrifce & non con altra.Et leuato un porcellio

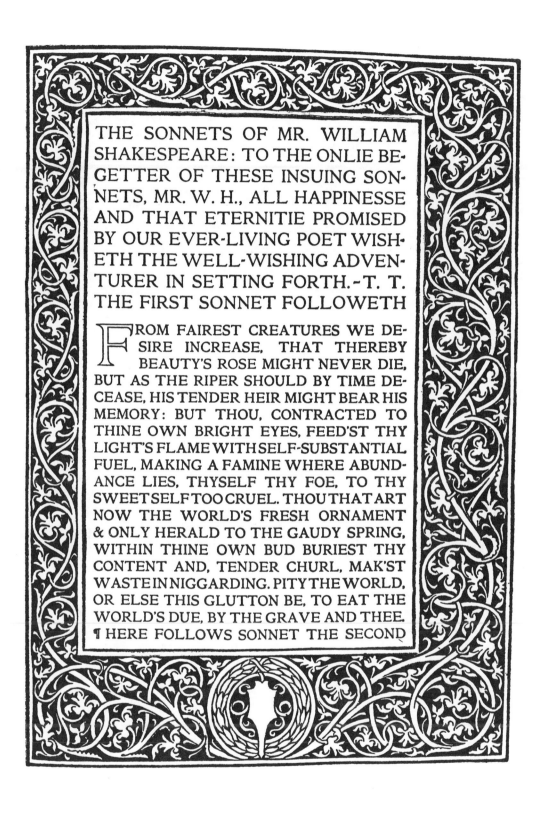

THE SONNETS OF MR. WILLIAM SHAKESPEARE: TO THE ONLIE BE-GETTER OF THESE INSUING SON-NETS, MR. W. H., ALL HAPPINESSE AND THAT ETERNITIE PROMISED BY OUR EVER-LIVING POET WISH-ETH THE WELL-WISHING ADVEN-TURER IN SETTING FORTH. ~ T. T. THE FIRST SONNET FOLLOWETH

FROM FAIREST CREATURES WE DE-SIRE INCREASE, THAT THEREBY BEAUTY'S ROSE MIGHT NEVER DIE, BUT AS THE RIPER SHOULD BY TIME DE-CEASE, HIS TENDER HEIR MIGHT BEAR HIS MEMORY: BUT THOU, CONTRACTED TO THINE OWN BRIGHT EYES, FEED'ST THY LIGHT'S FLAME WITH SELF-SUBSTANTIAL FUEL, MAKING A FAMINE WHERE ABUND-ANCE LIES, THYSELF THY FOE, TO THY SWEET SELF TOO CRUEL. THOU THAT ART NOW THE WORLD'S FRESH ORNAMENT & ONLY HERALD TO THE GAUDY SPRING, WITHIN THINE OWN BUD BURIEST THY CONTENT AND, TENDER CHURL, MAK'ST WASTE IN NIGGARDING. PITY THE WORLD, OR ELSE THIS GLUTTON BE, TO EAT THE WORLD'S DUE, BY THE GRAVE AND THEE. ¶ HERE FOLLOWS SONNET THE SECOND

RICCARDI PRESS: PAGE FROM "SONNETS OF SHAKESPEARE" PRINTED IN 14 AND 11 POINT CAPITALS DESIGNED BY HERBERT P. HORNE. BORDER FROM BERNARD PICTOR AND ERHARDT RATDOLT'S" APPIANUS," 1477

Marius the Epicurean

stream of moving lights across the white Forum, up the great stairs, to the palace. And, in effect, that night winter began, the hardest that had been known for a lifetime. The wolves came from the mountains; and, led by the carrion scent, devoured the dead bodies which had been hastily buried during the plague, and, emboldened by their meal, crept, before the short day was well past, over the walls of the farmyards of the Campagna. The eagles were seen driving the flocks of smaller birds across the dusky sky. Only, in the city itself the winter was all the brighter for the contrast, among those who could pay for light and warmth. The habitmakers made a great sale of the spoil of all such furry creatures as had escaped wolves and eagles, for presents at the 'Saturnalia'; and at no time had the winter roses from Carthage seemed more lustrously yellow and red.

CHAPTER XIII. THE 'MISTRESS AND MOTHER' OF PALACES

AFTER that sharp, brief winter, the sun was already at work, softening leaf and bud, as you might feel by a faint sweetness in the air; but he did his work behind an evenly white sky, against which the abode of the Cæsars, its cypresses and bronze roofs, seemed like a picture in beautiful but melancholy colour, as Marius climbed the long flights of steps to be introduced to the emperor Aurelius. Attired in the newest mode, his legs wound in dainty 'fasciæ' of white leather, with the heavy gold ring of the 'ingenuus,' and in his toga of ceremony, he still retained all his country freshness of complexion. The eyes of the 'golden youth' of Rome were upon him as the chosen friend of Cornelius, and the destined servant of the emperor; but not jealously. In spite of, perhaps partly because of, his habitual reserve of manner, he had become 'the fashion,' even among those who felt instinctively the irony which lay beneath that remarkable self-possession, as of one taking all things with a difference from other people, perceptible in voice, in expression, and even in his dress. It was, in truth, the air of one who, entering vividly into life, and relishing to the full the delicacies of its intercourse, yet feels all the while, from the point

RICCARDI PRESS : PAGE FROM WALTER PATER'S " MARIUS THE EPICUREAN,"
PRINTED IN 11 POINT FOUNT DESIGNED BY HERBERT P. HORNE

CAPITVLVM VI. INTERROGATIO DE EX-
ERCITIO ANTE COMMVNIONEM
VOX DISCIPVLI

CVM TVAM DIGNITATEM, DOMI-
ne, et meam uilitatem penso, ualde contremi-
sco et in me ipso confundor. Si enim non ac-
cedo uitam fugio, et si indigne me ingessero
offensam incurro. Quid ergo faciam, Deus meus, auxi-
liator meus in necessitatibus meis? Tu doce me uiam
rectam, propone breue aliquod exercitium sacrae com-
munioni congruum. Vtile est enim scire qualiter scili-
cet deuote ac reuerenter tibi praeparare debeo cor me-
um ad recipiendum salubriter tuum sacramentum, seu
etiam celebrandum tam magnum et diuinum sacrifici-
um.

CAPITVLVM VII. DE DISCVSSIONE PRO-
PRIAE CONSCIENTIAE ET EMENDATI-
ONIS PROPOSITO
VOX DILECTI

SVPER OMNIA CVM SVMMA HVMILI-
tate cordis et supplici reuerentia, cum plena fide
et pia intentione honoris Dei ad hoc sacramentum
celebrandum tractandum et sumendum oportet
Dei sacerdotem accedere. Diligenter examina consci-
entiam tuam, et pro posse tuo uera contritione et humili
confessione eam munda et clarifica, ita ut nil graue habeas aut scias quod te remordeat et liberum accessum
impediat. Habeas displicentiam omnium peccatorum
tuorum in generali, et pro quotidianis excessibus magis
in speciali doleas et gemas. Et si tempus patitur, Deo
in secreto cordis cunctas confitere passionum tuarum
miserias. Ingemisce et dole quod ita carnalis adhuc es
et mundanus, tam immortificatus a passionibus, tam
plenus concupiscentiarum motibus, tam incustoditus

ABERDEEN UNIVERSITY PRESS: PAGE FROM THE "DE IMITATIONE
CHRISTI" PRINTED IN THE "EWELL" TYPE DESIGNED BY DOUGLAS
COCKERELL FOR MESSRS. METHUEN AND CO.

XXXII. How the Worm came to the Howe, and how he was robbed of a cup; and how he fell on the folk.

NOT at all with self-wielding the craft of the worm-hoards
He sought of his own will, who sore himself harmed;
But for threat of oppression a thrall, of I wot not
Which bairn of mankind, from blows wrathful fled,
House-needy forsooth, and hied him therein,
A man by guilt troubled. Then soon it betided
That therein to the guest there stood grisly terror;
However the wretched, of every hope waning

.   .   .   .

The ill-shapen wight, whenas the fear gat him,
The treasure-vat saw; of such there was a many
Up in that earth-house of treasures of old,
As them in the yore-days, though what man I know not,
The huge leavings and loom of a kindred of high ones,
Well thinking of thoughts there had hidden away,
Dear treasures. But all them had death borne away
In the times of erewhile; and the one at the last
Of the doughty of that folk that there longest lived,
There waxed he friend-sad, yet ween'd he to tarry,
That he for a little those treasures the longsome
Might brook for himself. But a burg now all ready
Wonn'd on the plain nigh the waves of the water,
New by a ness, by narrow-crafts fasten'd;
Within there then bare of the treasures of earls
That herd of the rings a deal hard to carry,
Of gold fair beplated, and few words he quoth:

33

NOTE BY WILLIAM MORRIS ON HIS AIMS IN FOUNDING THE KELMSCOTT PRESS.

I BEGAN printing books with the hope of producing some which would have a definite claim to beauty, while at the same time they should be easy to read and should not dazzle the eye, or trouble the intellect of the reader by eccentricity of form in the letters. I have always been a great admirer of the calligraphy of the Middle Ages, & of the earlier printing which took its place. As to the fifteenth-century books, I had noticed that they were always beautiful by force of the mere typography, even without the added ornament, with which many of them are so lavishly supplied. And it was the essence of my undertaking to produce books which it would be a pleasure to look upon as pieces of printing and arrangement of type. Looking at my adventure from this point of view then, I found I had to consider chiefly the following things: the paper, the form of the type, the relative spacing of the letters, the words, and the

SICCOME DICE IL FILOSOFO NEL PRINCIPIO della Prima Filosofia 'tutti gli uomini naturalmente desiderano di sapere.' La ragione di che puote essere, che ciascuna cosa, da provvidenza di propria natura impinta, è inclinabile alla sua perfezione. Onde, acciocchè la scienza è l'ultima perfezione della nostra anima, nella quale sta la nostra ultima felicità, tutti naturalmente al suo desiderio siamo soggetti. Veramente da questa nobilissima perfezione molti sono privati per diverse cagioni che dentro dall'uomo, e di fuori da esso, lui rimuovono dall'abito di scienza. ⊏Dentro dall'uomo possono essere due difetti e impedimenti: l'uno dalla parte del corpo, l'altro dalla parte dell'anima. Dalla parte del corpo è, quando le parti sono indebitamente disposte, sicchè nulla ricevere può; siccome sono sordi & muti, e loro simili. Dalla parte dell'anima è, quando la malizia vince in essa, sicchè si fa seguitatrice di viziose dilettazioni, nelle quali riceve tanto inganno, che per quelle ogni cosa tiene a vile. Di fuori dall'uomo possono essere similmente due cagioni intese, l'una delle quali è induttrice di necessità, l'altra di pigrizia. La prima è la cura famigliare & civile, la quale convenevolmente a sè tiene degli uomini il maggior numero, sicchè in ozio di speculazione essere non possono. L'altra è il difetto del luogo ove la persona è nata e nudrita, che talora sarà da ogni studio non solamente privato, ma da gente studiosa lontano. ⊏Le due prime di queste cagioni, cioè la prima dalla parte di dentro & la prima dalla parte di fuori, non sono da vituperare, ma da scusare & di perdono degne; le due altre, avvegnachè l'una più, sono degne di biasimo e d'abominazione. Manifestamente adunqʒ può vedere chi bene considera, che pochi rimangono quelli che all'abito da tutti desiderato possano pervenire, & innumerabili quasi sono gl'impediti, che di questo cibo da tutti sempre vivono affamati. O beati que' pochi che seggono a quella mensa ove il pane degli Angeli si mangia, e miseri quelli che colle pecore hanno comune cibo!

ASHENDENE PRESS: PAGE PRINTED IN GREAT PRIMER TYPE MODELLED UPON THE TYPE USED BY SWEYNHEIM AND PANNARTZ AT SUBIACO IN 1465

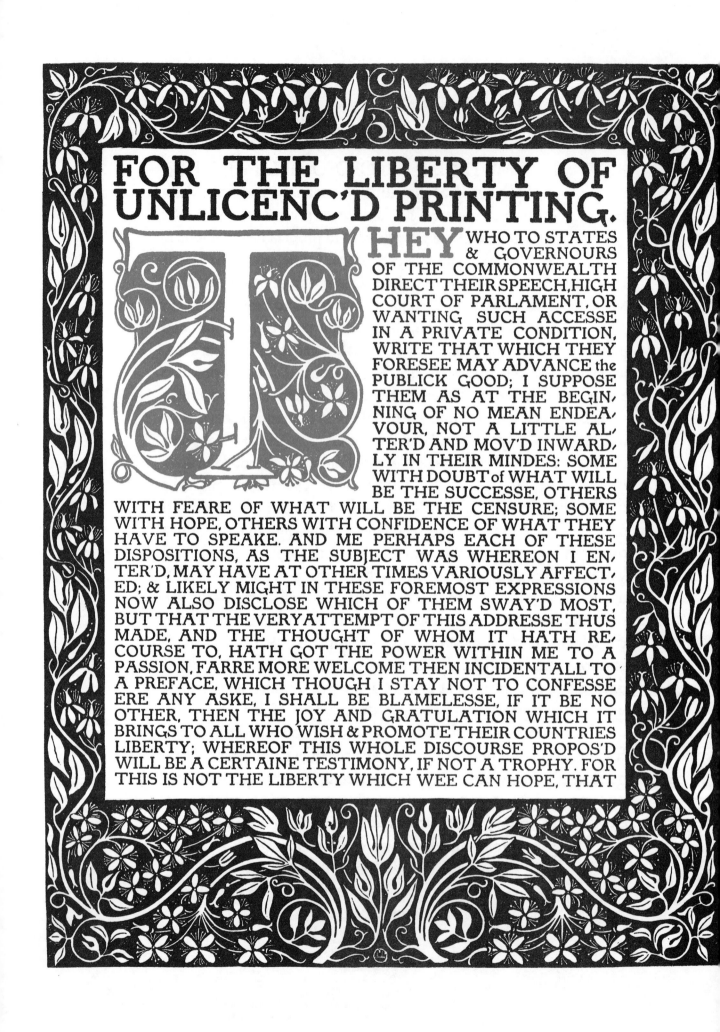

FOR THE LIBERTY OF UNLICENC'D PRINTING.

THEY WHO TO STATES & GOVERNOURS OF THE COMMONWEALTH DIRECT THEIR SPEECH, HIGH COURT OF PARLAMENT, OR WANTING SUCH ACCESSE IN A PRIVATE CONDITION, WRITE THAT WHICH THEY FORESEE MAY ADVANCE the PUBLICK GOOD; I SUPPOSE THEM AS AT THE BEGIN-NING OF NO MEAN ENDEA-VOUR, NOT A LITTLE AL-TER'D AND MOV'D INWARD-LY IN THEIR MINDES: SOME WITH DOUBT of WHAT WILL BE THE SUCCESSE, OTHERS WITH FEARE OF WHAT WILL BE THE CENSURE; SOME WITH HOPE, OTHERS WITH CONFIDENCE OF WHAT THEY HAVE TO SPEAKE. AND ME PERHAPS EACH OF THESE DISPOSITIONS, AS THE SUBJECT WAS WHEREON I EN-TER'D, MAY HAVE AT OTHER TIMES VARIOUSLY AFFECT-ED; & LIKELY MIGHT IN THESE FOREMOST EXPRESSIONS NOW ALSO DISCLOSE WHICH OF THEM SWAY'D MOST, BUT THAT THE VERY ATTEMPT OF THIS ADDRESSE THUS MADE, AND THE THOUGHT OF WHOM IT HATH RE-COURSE TO, HATH GOT THE POWER WITHIN ME TO A PASSION, FARRE MORE WELCOME THEN INCIDENTALL TO A PREFACE, WHICH THOUGH I STAY NOT TO CONFESSE ERE ANY ASKE, I SHALL BE BLAMELESSE, IF IT BE NO OTHER, THEN THE JOY AND GRATULATION WHICH IT BRINGS TO ALL WHO WISH & PROMOTE THEIR COUNTRIES LIBERTY; WHEREOF THIS WHOLE DISCOURSE PROPOS'D WILL BE A CERTAINE TESTIMONY, IF NOT A TROPHY. FOR THIS IS NOT THE LIBERTY WHICH WEE CAN HOPE, THAT

ERAGNY PRESS: OPENING PAGE OF THE "AREOPAGITICA" PRINTED IN THE "BROOK" TYPE, WITH BORDER AND INITIAL LETTER DESIGNED BY LUCIEN PISSARRO

From
The
Forest

XVII. THAT WOMEN ARE BUT MEN'S SHADDOWES.

OLLOW a shaddow, it still flies
    you,
        Seeme to flye it, it will pursue:
So court a mistris, shee denyes you;
Let her alone, shee will court you.
Say are not women truely, then,
Stil'd but shaddowes of us men?

At morne, and even, shades are longest;
At noone, they are or short, or none:
So men at weakest, they are strongest,
But grant us perfect, they're not knowne
Say, are not women truly, then,
Stil'd but shaddowes of us men?

From
The
Forest

XVIII. TO CELIA.

RINKE to me, onely with thine
    eyes,
        And I will pledge with mine:
Or leave a kisse but in the cup,
And Ile not looke for wine.
The thirst, that from the soule doth rise,
Doth aske a drinke divine:
But might I of Jove's Nectar sup.
I would not change for thine.
I sent thee, late, a rosie wreath,
Not so much honoring thee,

24

As giving it a hope, that there
It could not withered bee.
But thou thereon did'st only breathe,
And sent'st it backe to mee:
Since when it growes, and smells, I sweare,
Not of itself, but thee.

From
Joseph
Ritson's
Collection
of English
Songs.
18th Cen-
tury air.

Drink to me on-ly with thine eyes, &

Drink to me on-ly with thine eyes, &

Drink to me on-ly with thine eyes, &

I will pledge with mine

I will pledge with mine

I will pledge with mine

25

ERAGNY PRESS: PAGES FROM "SONGS BY BEN JONSON" PRINTED IN THE "BROOK" TYPE DESIGNED BY LUCIEN PISSARRO

CHRISTABEL.
PART THE FIRST.

'TIS THE MIDDLE OF NIGHT BY THE
CASTLE CLOCK,
AND THE OWLS HAVE AWAK-
ENED THE CROWING COCK,
TU—WHIT!——TU WHOO!
AND HARK, AGAIN! THE CROW-
ING COCK,
HOW DROWSILY IT CREW.

FROM BOCCACCIO'S LETTER TO PE-
TRARCH, DESCRIBING HIS VISIT TO
FRANCESCA, PETRARCH'S DAUGHTER,
AT VENICE, IN THE YEAR MCCCLXVII,
& TELLING OF ELETTA, FRANCESCA'S
LITTLE DAUGHTER.

WE sat chatting in your garden, and some of your friends who were there joined in the talk. Francesca most graciously pressed me to make myself at home, and proffered me your books & all your belongings, - all she had I was to consider mine; but not for a moment did she forget the modest demeanour of the perfect wife. She was welcoming me, when, lo, there before me was your dear little Eletta, my little friend! How gracefully she came along! One could not have expected such grace in so young a child. Before she could know who I was, she smiled at me so sweetly. What joy was mine when I saw her! What a hunger seized my heart as I held her in my arms! At first I thought it was my own girlie - the little maid once mine. Need I say more? You'll hardly believe me. But ask Doctor William of Ravenna and our friend Donatus. They know. Your little Eletta is the very image of my lost one. She has the same laugh, the

c

FLORENCE PRESS: PAGE FROM BOCCACCIO'S "OLYMPIA" SET IN ENGLISH
TYPE DESIGNED BY HERBERT P. HORNE, AND PRINTED AT THE ARDEN PRESS,
LETCHWORTH, FOR MESSRS. CHATTO AND WINDUS

A NOTE ON THE SPECIMENS OF LETTERING, ILLUMINATION, PRINTING AND BOOKBINDING SHOWN AT THE EXHIBITION OF ARTS AND CRAFTS HELD AT THE NEW GROSVENOR GALLERY, BOND STREET, W.

T the Arts and Crafts Exhibition nothing gives such complete satisfaction as the fine examples of writing done by Mr. Edward Johnston and by Mr. Graily Hewitt, and by other disciples of the school of lettering of which he is the founder. The importance of these exhibits is, of course, not to be measured by the beauty of the specimens themselves, although in many cases that is very great indeed. If we encourage fine writing, it is not because we wish to hang on our walls written and gilded texts from the Psalms or to treasure in our cabinets finely illuminated passages from Keats or the book of Job; it is because fine writing will give us fine lettering, wherever letter is used, whether in our printed books, or on the hoardings in the streets, or in the advertisement columns of our newspapers, or on the monuments and memorials in our graveyards and churches. The glory of the school is that the fine lettering which is taught there has already begun to penetrate to all these places. It is also finding its way into typefounders' specimen books, and it is well for the future of English printing that it should do so. Just as in the first years of printing the typefounders produced beautiful letter, because the fine writing of their day gave them their inspiration and their models, so in this modern school of writing we have the best hope for the inspiration and the models which will enable our typefounders to give us fine letter in the future. The value of the work of the school to the printer is shown at the Exhibition in the versal and initial letters written for the splendid quarto Virgil printed at the Ashendene Press by Mr. Hornby, in the fine books from the Doves Press, in the framed exhibit of type-letter designed by Miss Zompolides and used at the Arden Press in printing their folio volume on "The Gold and Silver of Windsor Castle." So far, however, the school has not produced a letter suitable for printing the text of a book. We feel sure that, if training and study be directed to that end, there may be designed under its influence founts of type-letter as graceful in the lower-case as in the majuscules, which shall fulfil all the requirements of modern printing. The true lines of development would seem to be those of the Italian humanistic letter of the fifteenth century, which gave the early printers their first roman letter.

Book illustration is not so well represented at the Exhibition as we should have wished. Many of the exhibits show a lack of the sympathy which should attach the drawing to the printed page which it is to accompany. It is, perhaps, difficult to bring the ordinary three-colour book

PAGE PRINTED IN THE "DOLPHIN OLD STYLE" TYPE, 12 POINT
DESIGNED AND CAST BY P. M. SHANKS AND SONS

40

OR DIENT ET CONTENT ET FABLENT

QUE LI QUENS BOUGARS DE VALENCE FAISOIT
guere au conte Garin de Biaucaire si grande et si mervel-
leuse et si mortel, qu'il ne fust uns seux jors ajornés qu'il ne
fust as portes et as murs et as bares de le vile a .c. cevaliers
et a .x. mile sergens a pié et a ceval; si li argoit sa terre et
gastoit son païs et ocioit ses homes. ¶ Li quens Garins de
Biaucaire estoit vix et frales si avoit son tans trespassé. Il
n'avoit nul oir, ne fil ne fille, fors un seul vallet. Cil estoit
tex con je vos dirai. Aucasins avoit a non li damoisiax; biax
estoit et gens et grans et bien tailliés de ganbes et de piés et
de cors et de bras. Il avoit les caviax blons et menus recer-
celés et les ex vairs et rians et le face clere et traitice et le
nes haut et bien assis, et si estoit enteciés de bones teces,
qu'en lui n'en avoit nule mauvaise, se bone non. Mais si
estoit soupris d'amor qui tout vaint, qu'il ne voloit estre
cevalers ne les armes prendre n'aler au tornoi ne fare point
de quanque il deust. Ses pere et se mere li disoient: ¶ Fix,
car pren tes armes si monte el ceval si deffént te terre et
aïe tes homes. S'il te voient entr'ex, si defenderont il mix
lor cors et le avoirs et te tere et le miue. ¶ Pere, fait Aucas-
sins, qu'en parlés vos ore? Ja dix ne me doinst riens que je
li demant, quant ere cevaliers ne monte a ceval, ne que voise
a estor ne a bataille, la u je fiere cevalier ni autres mi, se vos
ne me donés Nicholete, me douce amie que je tant aim.
¶ Fix, fait li peres, ce ne poroit estre. Nicolete laise ester;
que ce est une caitive qui fu amenee d'estrange terre, si

LONDON COUNTY COUNCIL CENTRAL SCHOOL OF ARTS AND CRAFTS: PAGE FROM "AUCASSIN
AND NICOLETTE," IN OLD FRENCH, PRINTED IN CASLON TYPE, WITH DECORATIVE HEADING

BOOK OPENING DESIGNED BY PERCY J. SMITH

I CHANCED UPON THE PRETTIEST, ODDEST FANTASTICAL THING OF A DREAM THE OTHER NIGHT, THAT YOU SHALL HEAR OF.

THE CHILD ANGEL ❖ ❖ A DREAM ❖ ❖ BY CHARLES LAMB

RICHARD BOTHS
NEUER KLEINER
REISEFÜHRER
DURCH PARISER
UND LONDONER
GALERIEN UND
MUSEEN

R. BOTH · PASING

THE "ANTIQUA" TYPE. DESIGNED BY PROF. PETER BEHRENS
CAST BY GEBR. KLINGSPOR, OFFENBACH A.M.

THE WISDOM OF CONFUCIUS

NEW YORK·R.H.RUSSELL·PUBLISHER·MDCCCCIII

THE WISDOM OF CONFUCIUS/ON DUTIES OF SONS

A BOY should never be allowed to see an instance of deceit. A lad should not wear a jacket of fur or the skirt. He must stand straight and square, and not incline his head in hearing. It is the rule for all sons that in the winter they should warm the bed for their parents, and to cool it in summer; in the evening to make everything ready, and to make inquiries in the morning. When with their companions they must not quarrel. When an older person is holding a boy by the hand, the boy should hold the elder's hand with both hands. When the elder has shifted his sword to the back and is speaking to him with his face bent down, the boy should cover his mouth with his hand in answering. When following one older they ascend to a level, he must keep his face toward the quarter to which the older is looking. When he has climbed to the wall of a city, he should not point

THE "ANTIQUA" TYPE. DESIGNED BY PROF. PETER BEHRENS CAST BY GEBR. KLINGSPOR, OFFENBACH A.M.

SENEFELDER
EN DE LITHOGRAFIE

Alois Senefelder, de uitvinder van het steendrukprocédé, was de zoon van een acteur. De oude heer Peter Senefelder had zich in München tot hoftooneelspeler weten op te werken. Daardoor ging Alois van zijn prilste jeugd af veel met tooneelspelers om en had hij zelf veel lust zich aan die edele kunst te wijden. Ter gelegenheid van een vastenavond, werd hem door eenige zijner vrienden verzocht een comediestuk te schrijven, waarin hijzelf eveneens een rol vervulde. Dit blijspel werd met bijzonder veel succes ontvangen en de jonge Alois verdiende er zijn eerste vijftig gulden mee.

Hij waande de gouden dagen reeds gekomen en besloot zich op het beroep van tooneelspeldichter toe te leggen.

Maar ook hier bleken de rozen niet zonder doornen te zijn.

De tweede poging van den jongen auteur werd met veel minder succes bekroond.

Ter nauwernood redde hij uit deze transactie de kosten van het drukken.

Maar één ding had hij ermee gewonnen, hij was tijdens het drukken van zijn stuk een beetje op de hoogte gekomen van de boekdrukkerij. En daaruit ontstond zijn besluit zichzelf een druk-

---

STUDIE-CLUB AMSTERDAM
TENTOONSTELLING 1913

CATALOGUS
DER TENTOONSTELLING
IN HET PALEIS VOOR VOLKS-
VLIJT-AMSTERDAM

Deze tentoonstelling is gedurende
elken werkdag geopend van af des
avonds vijf tot acht uur

THE "MEDIÆVAL" TYPE. DESIGNED BY PROF. PETER BEHRENS
CAST BY GEBR. KLINGSPOR, OFFENBACH A.M.

ŒUVRES
DE
J. RACINE
DE L'ACADÉMIE FRANÇAISE

NOUVELLE ÉDITION
PLUS CORRECTE ET PLUS
AMPLE QUE LES
PRÉCÉDENTES

TOME
II

A PARIS, CHEZ MUSIER FILS, QUAI
DES AUGUSTINS A SAINT ÉTIENNE

MITHRIDATE

TRAGÉDIE

ACTE I

SCÈNE PREMIÈRE
XIPHARÈS, ARBATE

XIPHARES

On nous faisait, Arbate, un fidèle rapport.
Rome en effet triomphe, et Mithridate est mort.
Les Romains, vers l'Euphrate, ont attaqué mon père,
Et trompé, dans la nuit, sa prudence ordinaire.
Après un long combat, tout son camp dispersé,
Dans la foule des morts, en fuyant, l'a laissé;
Et j'ai su qu'un soldat, dans les mains de Pompée,
Avec son diadème a remis son épée.
Ainsi, ce Roi, qui seul a, durant quarante ans,
Lassé tout ce que Rome eut de Chefs importants,
Et qui, dans l'Orient balançant la fortune,
Vengeait de tous les Rois la querelle commune,
Meurt, et laisse après lui, pour venger son trépas,
Deux fils infortunés qui ne s'accordent pas.

ARBATE

Vous, Seigneur! Quoi! l'ardeur de régner en sa place
Rend déjà Xipharès ennemi de Pharnace?

XIPHARES

Non, je ne prétends point, cher Arbate, à ce prix,
D'un malheureux Empire acheter le débris.
Je sais en lui des ans respecter l'avantage;
Et content des États marqués pour mon partage,
Je verrai, sans regret, tomber entre ses mains

THE "MEDIÆVAL" TYPE. DESIGNED BY PROF. PETER BEHRENS
CAST BY GEBR. KLINGSPOR, OFFENBACH A.M.

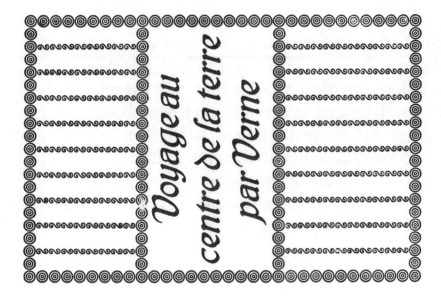

THE "KURSIV" TYPE. DESIGNED BY PROF. PETER BEHRENS
CAST BY GEBR. KLINGSPOR, OFFENBACH A.M.

Planeten=Kalendarium ✤

✤ eingerichtet auf das Jahr des Heils 1908.
Ein gar finnreich Büchlein über die Natur der
Planeten und deren Influenz und sonstige lehr=
same Dinge, mit Bauern=Praktika und Regeln
für den Menschen insgemein versehen. Ge=
zieret mit artigen Bildlein, so Meister
Sebald Beham von Nürenberg in
Holz geschnitten.
Zusammengestellt von
Marie von Redwitz

1908 ✤ Insel=Verlag in Leipzig

A GERMAN TYPE DESIGNED BY RUDOLF KOCH
CAST BY GEBR. KLINGSPOR, OFFENBACH A.M.

A NOTE ON THE SPECIMENS OF LETTERING, ILLUMI-
NATION, PRINTING AND BOOKBINDING SHOWN AT
THE EXHIBITION OF ARTS & CRAFTS HELD AT THE
NEW GROSVENOR GALLERY, BOND ST., LONDON, W.

T the Exhibition of Arts and Crafts nothing gives such complete satisfaction as the fine specimens of writing done by Mr. Edward Johnston and by Mr. Graily Hewitt, and other disciples of the school of lettering which he has established. The importance of these exhibits is, of course, not to be gauged by the actual beauty of the specimens themselves, though in many cases that is very great indeed. If we encourage fine writing, it is not because we wish to hang on our walls written and gilded texts from the Psalms, or to treasure in our cabinets finely illuminated passages from Keats or from the Book of Job; it is because fine writing will give us fine lettering, wherever lettering is used, whether in our printed books, or on the hoardings in the streets, or in the advertisement columns of our newspapers, or on the monuments and memorials in our graveyards and churches. It is the chief glory of the school that the fine lettering which is taught there has already begun to penetrate to all these places. It is also finding its way into the typefounders' specimen books, and it is well for the future of printing that it should do so. Just as in the first years of printing the typefounders produced beautiful letter because the fine writing of their day gave them their inspiration and their models, so in this modern school of writing we have the best hope for the inspiration and the models which will enable our typefounders to give us fine letter in the future. The value of the work of the school to the printer is shown at the Grosvenor Gallery in the versal and initial letters written for the splendid quarto Virgil printed by Mr. Hornby at the Ashendene Press, in the fine books from the Doves Press, in the exhibit of type-letter designed by Miss Zompolides and used at the Arden Press in printing their folio volume on "The Gold and Silver of Windsor Castle," and in other works of merit.

PAGE PRINTED IN THE "KENNERLEY" TYPE, 14 POINT, DESIGNED BY FREDERICK
W. GOUDY AND CAST BY H. W. CASLON AND CO. LTD. INITIAL LETTER BY
PAUL WOODROFFE, LENT BY THE ARDEN PRESS

ΟΔΥΣΣΕΙΑΣ ΒΙΒΛΟΣ ΔΕΥΤΕΡΑ. ΙΘΑ-
ΚΗΣΙΩΝ ΑΓΟΡΑ. ΤΗΛΕΜΑΧΟΥ ΑΠΟ-
ΔΗΜΙΑ.

Ἦμος δ᾽ ἠριγένεια φάνη ῥοδοδάκτυλος Ἠώς,
ὤρνυτ᾽ ἄρ᾽ ἐξ εὐνῆφιν Ὀδυσσῆος φίλος υἱός,
εἵματα ἐσσάμενος, περὶ δὲ ξίφος ὀξὺ θέτ᾽ ὤμῳ,
ποσσὶ δ᾽ ὑπὸ λιπαροῖσιν ἐδήσατο καλὰ πέδιλα,
βῆ δ᾽ ἴμεν ἐκ θαλάμοιο θεῷ ἐναλίγκιος ἄντην.
αἶψα δὲ κηρύκεσσι λιγυφθόγγοισι κέλευσε
κηρύσσειν ἀγορήνδε κάρη κομόωντας Ἀχαιούς.
οἱ μὲν ἐκήρυσσον, τοὶ δ᾽ ἠγείροντο μάλ᾽ ὦκα.
αὐτὰρ ἐπεί ῥ᾽ ἤγερθεν ὁμηγερέες τ᾽ ἐγένοντο,
βῆ ῥ᾽ ἴμεν εἰς ἀγορήν, παλάμῃ δ᾽ ἔχε χάλκεον ἔγχος,
οὐκ οἶος, ἅμα τῷ γε κύνες πόδας ἀργοὶ ἕποντο.
θεσπεσίην δ᾽ ἄρα τῷ γε χάριν κατέχευεν Ἀθήνη.
τὸν δ᾽ ἄρα πάντες λαοὶ ἐπερχόμενον θηεῦντο·
ἕζετο δ᾽ ἐν πατρὸς θώκῳ, εἶξαν δὲ γέροντες.
τοῖσι δ᾽ ἔπειθ᾽ ἥρως Αἰγύπτιος ἦρχ᾽ ἀγορεύειν,
ὃς δὴ γήραϊ κυφὸς ἔην καὶ μυρία ᾔδη.
καὶ γὰρ τοῦ φίλος υἱὸς ἅμ᾽ ἀντιθέῳ Ὀδυσῆϊ
Ἴλιον εἰς εὔπωλον ἔβη κοίλῃς ἐνὶ νηυσίν,
Ἄντιφος αἰχμητής· τὸν δ᾽ ἄγριος ἔκτανε Κύκλωψ
ἐν σπῆϊ γλαφυρῷ, πύματον δ᾽ ὡπλίσσατο δόρπον.
τρεῖς δέ οἱ ἄλλοι ἔσαν, καὶ ὁ μὲν μνηστῆρσιν ὁμίλει,
Εὐρύνομος, δύο δ᾽ αἰὲν ἔχον πατρώϊα ἔργα·
ἀλλ᾽ οὐδ᾽ ὣς τοῦ λήθετ᾽ ὀδυρόμενος καὶ ἀχεύων.
τοῦ ὅ γε δάκρυ χέων ἀγορήσατο καὶ μετέειπε·

OXFORD UNIVERSITY PRESS: PAGE FROM THE "ODYSSEY," PRINTED
IN THE "OTTER" TYPE DESIGNED BY ROBERT W. PROCTOR

LOVE that long since hast to thy mighty powre
Perforce subdude my poore captived hart,
And, raging now therein with restlesse stowre,
Doest tyrannize in everie weaker part;
Faine would I seeke to ease my bitter smart
By any service I might do to thee,
Or ought that else might to thee pleasing be.

And now t' asswage the force of this new flame,
And make thee more propitious in my need,
I meane to sing the praises of thy name,
And thy victorious conquests to areed,
By which thou madest many harts to bleed
Of mighty Victors, with wyde wounds embrewed,
And by thy cruell darts to thee subdewed.

Onely I feare my wits enfeebled late
Through the sharpe sorrowes which thou hast me bred,
Should faint, and words should faile me to relate
The wondrous triumphs of my great god-hed:
But, if thou wouldst vouchsafe to overspred
Me with the shadow of thy gentle wing,
I should enabled be thy actes to sing.

Come, then, O come, thou mightie God of Love,
Out of thy silver bowres and secret blisse,
Where thou doest sit in Venus lap above,
Bathing thy wings in her ambrosiall kisse,
That sweeter farre then any Nectar is;
Come softly, and my feeble breast inspire
With gentle furie, kindled of thy fire.

LONDON COUNTY COUNCIL CENTRAL SCHOOL OF ARTS AND CRAFTS: PAGE FROM
EDMUND SPENSER'S " FOUR HYMNS ON EARTHLY AND HEAVENLY LOVE AND BEAUTY"
PRINTED IN CASLON TYPE. WOODCUT INITIAL BY W. F. NORTHEND, STUDENT

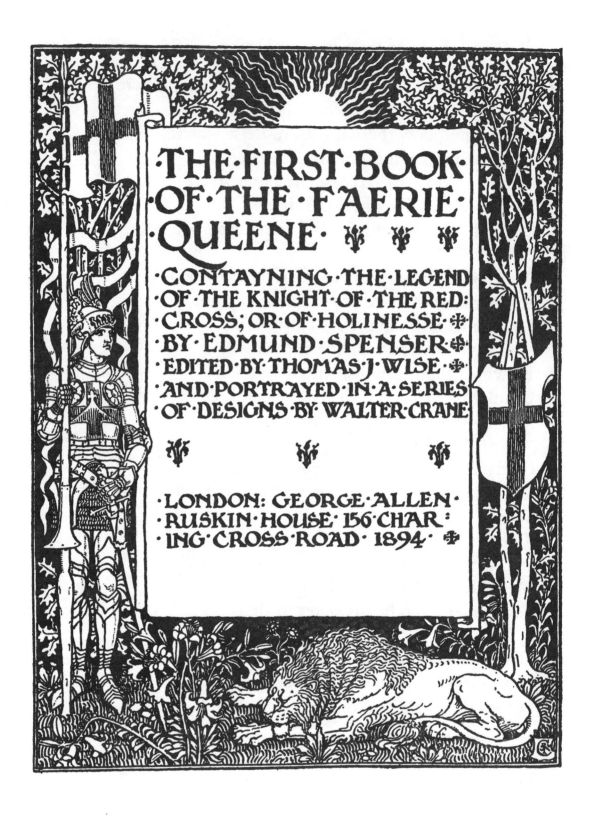

54

The Patron of true Holinesse
Foule Errour doth defeate;
Hypocrisie, him to entrappe,
Doth to his home entreate.

FULL-PAGE ILLUSTRATION BY WALTER CRANE FOR
THE FIRST BOOK OF "THE FAERIE QUEENE." (SIZE
OF ORIGINAL WOOD-ENGRAVING 9¼×7¼ INCHES)

REIGATE PRESS: TITLE AND OPENING PAGES DESIGNED BY W. BERNARD ADENEY

TALES from the NORSE

With Pictures

6 Reginald L. Knowles
& Horace J. Knowles

DESIGN FOR A TITLE-PAGE. BY REGINALD L. KNOWLES.
PUBLISHED BY MESSRS. GEORGE ROUTLEDGE AND SONS, LTD.

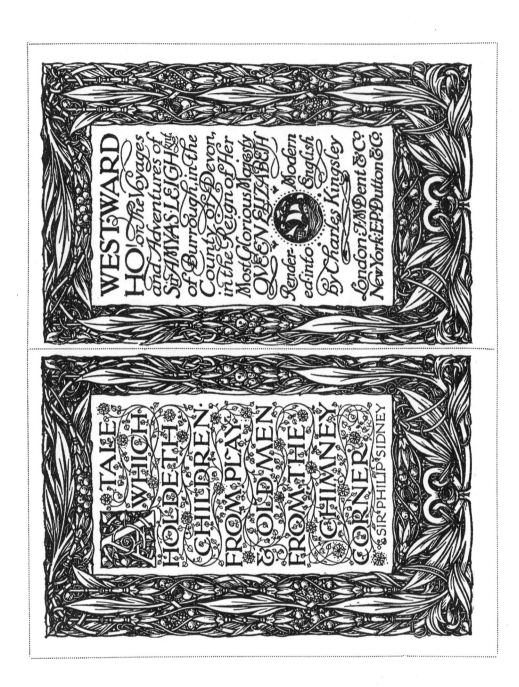

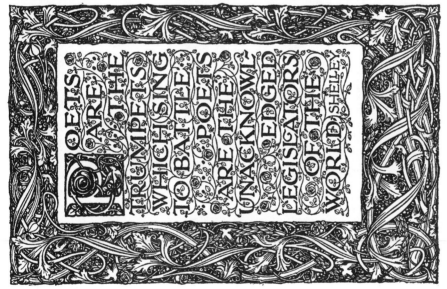

TITLE-PAGE OPENING OF THE POETRY SECTION OF "EVERYMAN'S LIBRARY"
DESIGNED BY REGINALD L. KNOWLES FOR MESSRS. J. M. DENT AND SONS LTD.

FRIENDSHIP
By
Clifford Bax

Published by B.T.Batsford.London

"Sometimes thou seem'st not as thyself alone
But as the meaning of all things that are."

I

ONCE on a certain cloudless day of July at the pleasant hour which falls about midway between noon and sunset, my work being finished I went out into the garden and lying there in the grass I wondered at the happiness of my life. Now when I questioned myself "What element in your life has seemed to you the most beautiful of all?" I realized that I must answer with the one word "Friendship." And then, like an astronomer who turns his telescope from star to star, I thought of the men and women whose temperaments and characters I have come to love and revere.

I

"FELLOWSHIP" BOOK. TITLE AND OPENING PAGES DESIGNED BY JAMES GUTHRIE LETTERING BY PERCY J. SMITH. PUBLISHED BY MESSRS. B. T. BATSFORD LTD.

DOMI MINA
NVS TIO
ILLV MEA

FRONTISPIECE TO AYMER VALLANCE'S "OLD COLLEGES OF OXFORD"
DESIGNED BY HAROLD NELSON FROM SUGGESTIONS BY AYMER VALLANCE
PUBLISHED BY MESSRS. B. T. BATSFORD LTD.

ANATOLE FRANCE

BEE

THE PRINCESS OF THE DWARFS

RETOLD IN ENGLISH BY PETER WRIGHT & ILLUSTRATED BY CHARLES ROBINSON

LONDON . J.M.Dent & Sons Ltd . Bedford St. W.C
NEW YORK , E.P.Dutton & Co
1912

TITLE-PAGE DESIGNED BY CHARLES ROBINSON
FOR MESSRS. J. M. DENT AND SONS LTD.

THE BIRTH LIFE AND ACTS OF KING ARTHUR OF HIS
NOBLE KNIGHTS OF THE ROUND TABLE THEIR
MARVELLOUS ENQUESTS AND ADVENTURES
THE ACHIEVING OF THE SAN GREAL
AND IN THE END LE MORTE DAR-
THUR WITH THE DOLOUROUS
DEATH AND DEPARTING
OUT OF THIS WORLD
OF THEM ALL.

THE TEXT AS WRIT-
TEN BY SIR THOMAS MALORY
AND IMPRINTED BY WILLIAM CAXTON
AT WESTMINSTER THE YEAR MCCCCLXXXV
AND NOW SPELLED IN MODERN STYLE.   WITH AN
INTRODUCTION BY PROFESSOR RHYS AND EMBELLISHED
WITH MANY ORIGINAL DESIGNS BY AUBREY BEARDSLEY.   MDCCCCIX.

TITLE-PAGE DESIGNED BY AUBREY BEARDSLEY
FOR MESSRS. J. M. DENT AND SONS LTD.

ROBIN HOOD AND GUY OF GISBORNE.

When shaws be sheene, and swards full fayre
And leaves both large and longe,
Itt is merrye walkyng in the fayre forrest
To heare the small birdes' songe.

The woodweele sang, and wold not cease,
Sitting upon the spraye,
Soe lowde, he wakened Robin Hood,
In the greenwood where he lay.

"Now, by my faye," said jollye Robin,
"A sweaven I had this night,
I dreamt me of two wight yemen,
That fast with me can fight.

Methought they did mee beate and binde,
And tooke my bowe mee froe;
Iff I be Robin alive in this lande,
Ile be wroken on them towe."

17

ILLUSTRATION AND PAGE OF TEXT FROM "ROBIN HOOD BALLADS." DESIGNED BY R. JAMES WILLIAMS. PUBLISHED BY THE VINCENT PRESS

CERVANTES

ODON QUICHOTTE

ILLUSTRATIONS DE THOMAS DERRICK

DESIGN FOR A TITLE-PAGE. BY THOMAS DERRICK
PUBLISHED BY MESSRS. SIEGLE, HILL AND CO.

Some things there are that have
been wrested from us
In our blind haste and
frenzy of employ,
Things that by right & for our
good belong us, —
Time to reflect & leisure
to enjoy

Oh Quiet Life, that with
unstudied measure,
Did ever bide in dusy's
grasp a Charm.
And ever linked with toil
a time of leisure.
Oh yield us still some
remnant of thy balm!

Fulbeck
A Pastoral
by
J. Walter West A.R.W.S.
With illustrations
by the Author

London.
A. Wilford Bell
Hastings House
Norfolk St:
Strand
1901

THE LOVER TELLS OF THE ROSE
IN HIS HEART

All things uncomely and broken,
all things worn and old,
The cry of a child by the road-
way the creak of a lumbering cart,
The heavy steps of the ploughman, splashing
the wintry mould,
Are wronging your image that blossoms a rose
in the deeps of my heart.

The wrong of unshapely things is a
wrong too great to be told;
I hunger to build them anew and sit
on a green knoll apart,
With the earth and the sky and the water,
remade, like a casket of gold
For my dreams of your image that blossoms
a rose in the deeps of my heart.

Cuala Press.   W·B·Yeats.

FINE BOOKBINDING IN ENGLAND.
BY DOUGLAS COCKERELL

FINE or " extra " binding as it is called in the trade implies that the craftsman has done his best with the best materials. It may be plain or decorated, but whatever work there is should be the best of which the craftsman is capable. Printed books are largely machine-made productions, and it would seem reasonable that machine-made books should have machine-made covers, and it is in such covers or "cases" that most of our books are issued. There is a general feeling that the cost of the binding should bear some relation to the cost of the book ; but since books are turned out by the thousand from the printing press, and fine bindings can only be made singly and laboriously by hand, it is inevitable that in most cases such a binding costs much more than the book it covers. This has probably been the case since the invention of printing cheapened books, and yet there have always been people who valued certain books highly enough to have them well bound and decorated. For a true book-lover does not value a book at the price it costs, and he may wish to have the words of a favourite author enshrined in a precious cover. Some books by their nature and use call for lavish treatment. Books used for important ceremonies, such as altar books or lectern Bibles, can quite well be covered with ornament, provided this ornament is good. They will be but a spot of gorgeousness in a great church or cathedral, and should be judged in relation to their surroundings and not as isolated articles. ✠ There is a fashion now to value decoration in inverse ratio to its quantity, and demand that it should be concentrated on spots, leaving the greater part of the surface of articles bare. This is quite a reasonable way to treat a binding, but it is not the only way. A satisfactory binding can be made with little or no ornament, and there is then little fear of a disastrous failure. To cover a book all over with gold-tooled decoration is a more difficult thing to do satisfactorily, but it can be done, and, if well done, is well worth doing. ✠ At the present time there are many binders working in England who are capable of turning out work of the highest class, and fortunately there are book-lovers here and in America with the taste and means to commission such work. Probably, if a man were bold enough to spend five or ten thousand pounds on binding the finest books that are being produced at the present time, he would find, if the money were wisely spent, that he had got a library that would be celebrated all over the world. There is an interesting revival in the use of arms-blocks on bindings, and when certain modern libraries come to be dispersed their owners will be remembered by their books in the same way as are the original owners of the many armorial bindings that have come down to us from the past. ✄ There are some qualities that are common to all well-bound books. Of course abnormal books have to be treated specially, but it may generally be said that every leaf of a book should open right to the back. This means that all single leaves and plates should be attached by guards, and that no overcasting or pasting-in should be allowed, and it also means that the back should be truly flexible. The sections should be sewn to flexible cords or tapes, the ends of these should be firmly attached to the boards, and the back should be covered with some flexible material, such as leather, which, while protecting the sewing-thread or cord, shall itself add to the strength of the binding. A fine binding will have many other features added by way of refinement or elaboration, but unless it has these qualities it is likely to be an unsatisfactory piece of work. A well-bound book should open well and stay open, and shut well and stay shut. The binder can bind any book so that it will not open, but there are some books that he cannot bind so that they will open and shut "sweetly." ✄ Bookbinding is only one part of the larger craft of book production, and to obtain a perfect book it is necessary that the workers in each branch of the craft should have a common ideal of what a book should be, and that each should do his part in such a way that this ideal may be attained. Unfortunately it too often happens that the printers are quite content if their printing looks perfect as it comes from the press, with the result —through errors in the choice of paper or the number of leaves to a section—that the bookbinder has unnecessary and sometimes unsurmountable obstacles put in his way. A book that will not open freely and that gapes like a dead oyster when it ought to be shut is not pleasant to use, and when these faults are noticed the binder generally gets the blame. Sometimes he deserves the blame, for the fault may be his, but more often than not the fault lies with the paper. To open a book a certain number of leaves of paper must be bent, and if the paper is so stiff that a single leaf will not fall over by its own weight, the book cannot be made to open quite satisfactorily if bound in the ordinary way. By swinging each leaf on a guard it is possible to bind a pack of playing-cards into something like a book which will open and shut freely, but that this *can* be done is no excuse for the production of books which necessitate this drastic treatment before they can be bound satisfactorily. ✄ William Morris, when he founded the Kelmscott Press, did more than revive fine book-printing ; he established a tradition for books that were eminently bindable, and the presses that followed his lead kept up the tradition ; so that we have in England a large number of beautifully printed books that are worthy of the best binding, and that impose no unnecessary difficulties on the binder. ✄ Mr. Cobden-Sanderson did much to revive the use of the tight or flexible back. In this style

76

the leather is attached directly to the back of the sections, and so helps to hold them firmly together. All leather-bound books had tight backs until about a hundred years ago, when the hollow back came into general use. A tight back should throw up when the book is opened ; that is to say the back, convex when the book is shut, should become concave on the book being opened. This causes a certain amount of creasing in the leather, and this creasing is not good for gold tooling ; but with a well-bound book the damage is not serious, and important constructional features must not be sacrificed for the sake of the decoration. ✠ The hollow back does not crease the leather, and so is preferred by finishers, and besides it is easier to cover a hollow back neatly than a tight one ; but the strain of opening and shutting, which should be distributed evenly across the back, is in the hollow back thrown on the joints, with the result that the leather is apt to break at these places unless specially strengthened, as is the case with well-bound account books. ✠ While "flexible" backs that are truly flexible are undoubtedly the best, some binders line up their backs so stiffly under the leather as to allow little or no movement when the book is opened. This avoids the creasing of the leather and leaves the decoration uninjured, but the book will not open freely, and there is no virtue in such a tight back. Leather is chosen for binding because of its toughness and flexibility, yet binders deliberately sacrifice this last quality in order to obtain extreme neatness or to hide faults in the forwarding. ✠ It is the fashion in some quarters to admire as the perfection of craftsmanship an exact and hard square edge to the boards of a book. This can only be got by paring the leather down till it is as thin as paper and has consequently very little strength. A softer, rounder edge is natural to a leather-covered article, and it is unreasonable to expect the qualities of a newly planed board in a material so wholly different in character. The edges of the leather-covered board should have a distinctly flat face, and clumsiness will be avoided by any good craftsman. It is only the extreme sharpness, so much admired by unknowing people, that is objectionable. ✠ In the treatment of the edges of the leaves fashion has gone to two extremes : some book-lovers demand that the edges should be entirely uncut, while others require them to look like a solid piece of metal. The rough edges, or "deckle," on handmade paper is a necessary defect due to the way the paper is made. These rough edges were always trimmed off by the early binders because they were unsightly, difficult to turn over, and harboured dust. Some of the shorter leaves would usually be left untrimmed. Such short leaves are known in the trade as "proof," *i.e.* proof that the book has not been unduly cut down. To gild a book-edge absolutely solid the binder must cut down to the shortest leaves and so often has to reduce the size of the book unreasonably ; but an acceptable compromise between entirely uncut edges and solid gilding can be arrived at if the sections of a book to be finely bound are trimmed singly and gilt " in the rough " before sewing. This enriches the edges but does not disguise their nature nor necessitate their being unduly cropped. ❦ In recent times there has been much good work done in England in the investigation of bookbinding materials. The Royal Society of Arts Committee on " Leather for Bookbinding " has established standards of leather that have made it possible for binders to procure skins that are uninjured in the process of manufacture, and bookbinding leather of the very highest class is now being produced in England. The leather manufacturers are able to dye leather any reasonable shade without the use of sulphuric acid, and it is only some of the lighter fancy colours that are unprocurable in "acid free" leather. That these "fancy" shades are unprocurable in uninjured leather is a distinct gain, as they mostly fade, and books bound in such leather seldom look as if they were intended to be used. ❦ There are various ways by which leather-bound books may be decorated, but tooling, either in gold or blind, is by far the commonest, and it is tooled bindings that we are considering here. " Blind" tooling is the impression of hot tools on the leather. The most satisfactory tools for blind work are those cut die-sunk like a seal. These, by depressing the ground, leave the ornament in relief. Tools for gold work are cut so that the ornament with the gold is depressed below the surface of the leather. These tools may be used without gold, but blind tooling produced in this way has little of the character associated with this work when it was at its best, *i.e.* up to the end of the fifteenth century. Gold-tooling came to Europe from the East, and preserved a tradition of Eastern design for a very long period. The English gold-tooled bindings of the seventeenth and eighteenth centuries are often strangely Eastern in the style of the decoration. ❦ The ornamentation of fine bindings reached almost its lowest ebb in England about the middle of last century. Of technical skill there was never any lack, but decoration had lost vitality, and the ornamental bindings of this time are for the most part copies or parodies of the work of earlier binders. William Morris designed a few very beautiful gold-tooled bindings which were covered all over with the impressions of tools, each one of which represented a complete plant. His friend, Mr. Cobden-Sanderson, who gave up the practice of the law to learn the binder's craft, produced books that are unsurpassed in the delicate beauty of their decoration. Before his time there had been few attempts to combine tools to form organic patterns. Mr. Cobden-Sanderson's tools were very elementary in character, each flower, leaf or bud being the impression of a separate tool. These impressions were combined in such a way as to give a sense of growth, and yet in no way overlapped the traditional limitations and conventions

78

of the craft. Mr. Cobden-Sanderson got his results by sheer genius in the right use of simple elements. He used inlays very sparingly, and his finest bindings depend entirely on the effect of gold on leather. The style of design which he founded has spread throughout the trade, mainly through the teaching at the various technical schools, and it is now comparatively rare to find an elaborate binding of recent date without some attempt having been made to connect the tools so that they together form an organic whole. ❧ The use of composite tools (that is, tools which form a whole design in themselves and do not bear any definite relationship to one another) is now restricted to cheap bindings. The corners and centres on the backs of school prizes are familiar, if degraded, examples of the use of such tools. Together with the Cobden-Sanderson style of decoration there has been a marked revival of the use of interlacement in gold-tooled designs. Interlaced gold lines, if not so intricate as to be bewildering, may be very beautiful, but in this, as in most other crafts, the highly-skilled workman loves to attempt the almost impossible, and some of the recent interlaced patterns fail on account of their over-elaboration and consequent restlessness. ❧ Mr. Charles Ricketts designed some very notable gold-tooled bindings for the Vale Press. These bindings have hardly received the attention they deserve, and the style has not spread to any extent, possibly because Mr. Ricketts' refinement and delicacy in the use of fine lines are not easy to acquire. These bindings have an architectural quality that places them in a class by themselves. Mr. Cobden-Sanderson and Mr. Ricketts, in their entirely different styles, have shown that gold-tooling may be extremely beautiful as decoration without overstepping the traditional limits of the craft, and in the case of the most successful bindings now being produced these traditional limits have been recognised. Gold-tooling is by its nature a limited means of expression, though exactly where the limits lie must be a matter of feeling and taste rather than of knowledge. Certainly in some of the elaborate bindings now being produced the limits of the craft have been passed, and while serving to show amazing dexterity on the part of the finisher, these bindings are less successful artistically than many that are less ambitious in technique. ❧ There is no clearly marked school of blind-tooling at present, though here and there the method has been used with success. Mr. William Morris designed a notable binding in white pigskin for the Kelmscott "Chaucer." Many copies were so bound at the Doves Bindery, but most of the attempts that have been made to carry out work in the same style have been comparatively unsuccessful. ❧ There have been a good many efforts made to revive modelled leather-work as a means of decorating books, but although this method is capable of producing very fine results, most of the binding in modelled leather shown in recent

79

exhibitions cannot be said to be successful. Any work that has to be done on the leather before the book is bound is almost doomed to failure, because leather which is modelled before binding cannot be handled by the binder with the freedom that is necessary if he is to make a workmanlike job of the covering. It is, however, possible to put quite sufficient relief in modelled leather after a book is bound, if the leather be reasonably thick; indeed high relief for most books is objectionable. ✠ Many of the old bindings had fine metal mounts and clasps. If clasps are used on modern books, as a rule they should be flush with the sides, so as not to scratch their neighbours when taken in and out of shelves. Raised clasps and bosses are only suitable for books that are expected to stand permanently on a lectern. ✠ In criticising decorated bindings there is a danger of falling into the common error of generalising from isolated instances. You cannot put too much ornament on a thing as small as a bookcover if the ornament is good enough. A book well bound in beautiful leather may be perfectly satisfactory and beautiful by virtue of good workmanship, fine material and colour. A binding covered with fine gold-tooling may be just as restful and far more beautiful, but while there is comparatively little scope for failure in the plain binding, there are appalling pitfalls if the cover be lavishly decorated. There are, of course, all sorts of degrees of decoration between an absolutely plain binding and one covered entirely with gold, but there are some qualities common to most successful tooled ornament. ✠ There are few bindings that are quite successful unless the ornament is arranged on a symmetrical plan. Any attempt to portray landscape, human figures or naturalistic flowers is almost doomed to failure. Gold-tooling is not a suitable medium for rendering such subjects. ✠ Lettering should be well designed and free from eccentricities. The problem of lettering a long title across a narrow back may necessitate ungainly breaking of words, but where this is done it should only be done from obvious necessity, and the reasonable necessity for this fault should be apparent. To letter books in type so small as to be quite illegible, lettering that looks from a short distance like a gold line, is more unreasonable than almost any breaking of words that allows the use of letters of a larger size. ✠ Fine binding is an expensive luxury but not an unreasonable one compared with many others. We have now in England a school of really fine binding, and the most reasonable and unobjectionable form that luxury can take is the use of beautiful things in everyday life. If a book is well bound and well decorated it is fit to use, and in choosing a book to be expensively bound it would be better to choose the book most often used than one which would be put away unopened. Most fine bindings would be greatly improved by use, and the reasonable using of them would give immense pleasure, a pleasure that would justify the binder's care and trouble and the purchaser's outlay. The use of a beautiful thing gives a far higher form of pleasure than does the mere sense of ownership.

80

BOOKBINDING IN BLUE PIGSKIN, WITH HERALDIC BORDER ENCLOSING A PANEL OF FLORAL DESIGN AND BACKGROUND OF POINTILLÉ. BY KATHARINE ADAMS

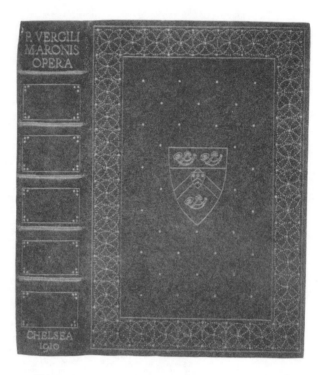

BOOKBINDING WITH GEOMETRICAL BORDER IN POINTILLÉ
BY KATHARINE ADAMS

BOOKBINDING IN BROWN MOROCCO, WITH INLAY, GOLD TOOLING, OAK
SIDES AND LEATHER CLASPS.   DESIGNED AND TOOLED BY L. HAY-COOPER
FORWARDED BY W. H. SMITH AND SON
(In the possession of the Grey Coat Hospital, Westminster)

BOOKBINDING IN GREEN MOROCCO, WITH INLAY AND GOLD TOOLING
DESIGNED AND TOOLED BY L. HAY-COOPER, BOUND BY S. BARNARD

BOOKBINDING IN DONKEY HIDE, WITH VELLUCENT PANEL AND GOLD TOOLING
DESIGNED BY O. CARLETON SMYTH, EXECUTED BY CEDRIC CHIVERS OF BATH

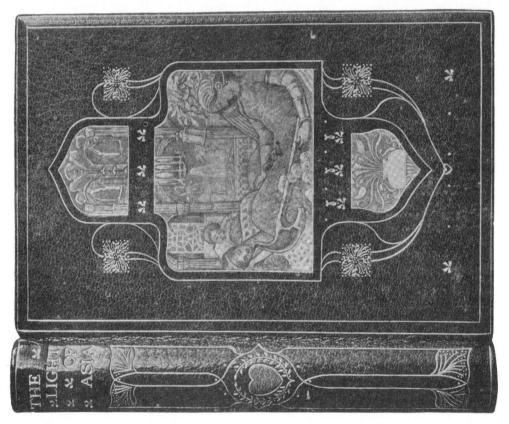

BOOKBINDING IN WHOLE CRUSHED CRIMSON LEVANT MOROCCO, WITH VELLUCENT
PANELS AND GOLD TOOLING. DESIGNED BY H. GRANVILLE FELL, EXECUTED BY
CEDRIC CHIVERS OF BATH

BOOKBINDING IN APPLE-GREEN LEVANT MOROCCO, WITH BLIND AND GOLD
TOOLING. BY R. DE COVERLY AND SONS

BOOKBINDING IN NIGER MOROCCO, WITH INLAY AND GOLD TOOLING
BY R. DE COVERLY AND SONS

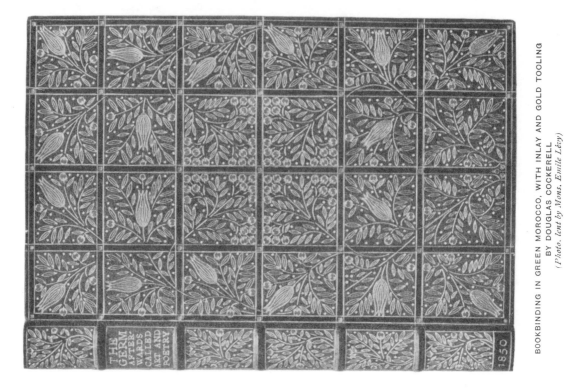

BOOKBINDING IN GREEN MOROCCO, WITH INLAY AND GOLD TOOLING
BY DOUGLAS COCKERELL
(Photo. lent by Mons. Emile Lévy)

BOOKBINDING IN GREEN MOROCCO, WITH INLAY AND GOLD TOOLING
BY DOUGLAS COCKERELL
(Photo. lent by Mons. Emile Lévy)

86

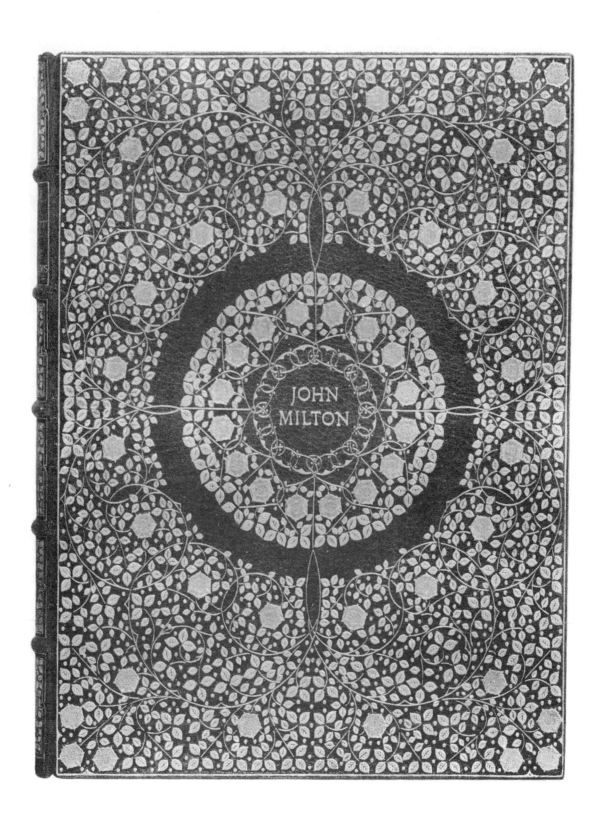

JOHN
MILTON

BOOKBINDING IN GREEN MOROCCO, WITH INLAY
AND GOLD TOOLING. BY DOUGLAS COCKERELL

*(Photo. lent by
Mons. Emile Lèvy)*

BOOKBINDING IN DARK RED MOROCCO, WITH INLAY
AND GOLD TOOLING. BY DOUGLAS COCKERELL

BOOKBINDING IN RED NIGER MOROCCO, WITH GOLD TOOLING
BY FRANK G. GARRETT

BOOKBINDING IN VELLUM, WITH GOLD AND GREEN TOOLING. BY FRANK G. GARRETT

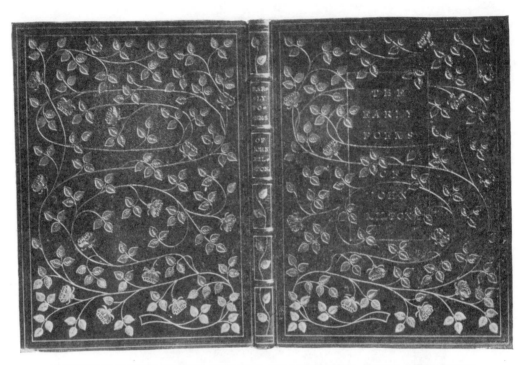

BOOKBINDING IN MAUVE MOROCCO, WITH INLAY AND GOLD TOOLING. BY HON. NORAH HEWITT

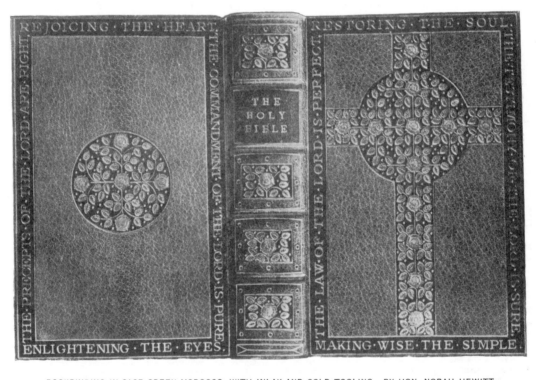

BOOKBINDING IN SAGE GREEN MOROCCO, WITH INLAY AND GOLD TOOLING. BY HON. NORAH HEWITT

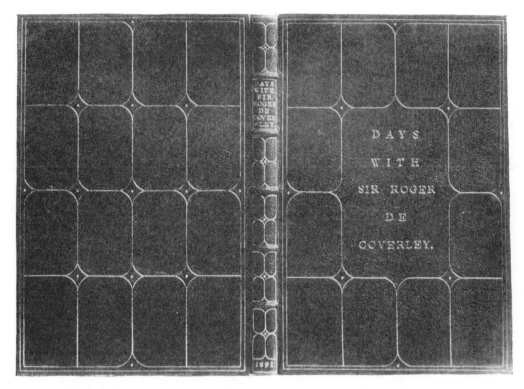

BOOKBINDING IN POWDER BLUE MOROCCO, WITH GOLD TOOLING. BY HON. NORAH HEWITT

BOOKBINDING IN NIGER MOROCCO, WITH GOLD TOOLING. BY HON. NORAH HEWITT

BOOKBINDING IN BLUE LEVANT MOROCCO, WITH INLAY AND GOLD TOOLING
DESIGNED BY T. TURBAYNE, EXECUTED BY J. GREEN (OXFORD UNIVERSITY PRESS)

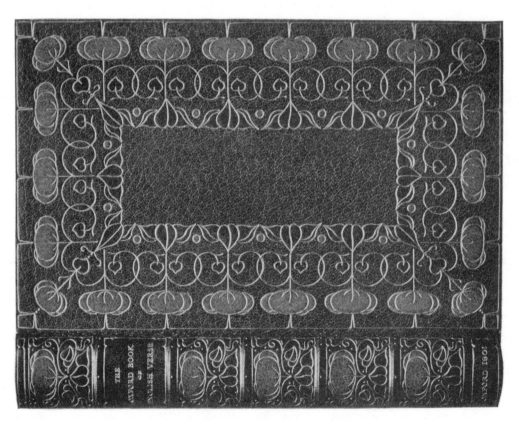

BOOKBINDING IN RED LEVANT MOROCCO, WITH INLAY AND GOLD TOOLING
DESIGNED BY J. GREEN, EXECUTED BY S. TOUT (OXFORD UNIVERSITY PRESS)

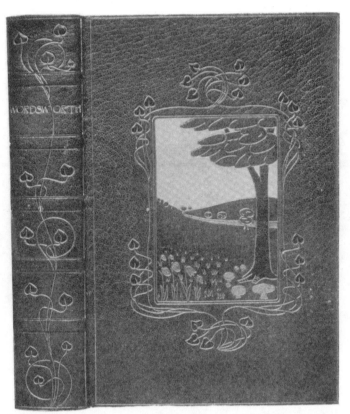

BOOKBINDING IN MAROON LEVANT MOROCCO, WITH INLAID PANEL. DESIGNED
BY J. GREEN, EXECUTED BY P. WARD (OXFORD UNIVERSITY PRESS)

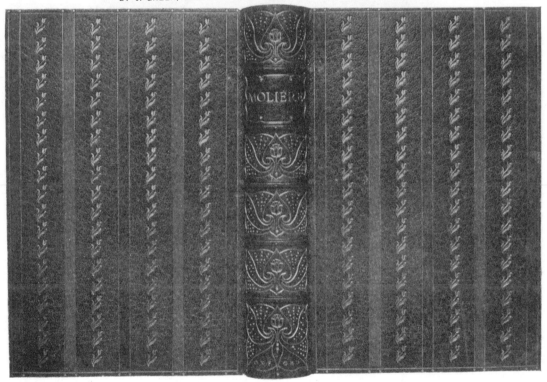

BOOKBINDING IN GREEN LEVANT MOROCCO, WITH GOLD TOOLING. DESIGNED BY T. TURBAYNE, EXECUTED BY P. WARD
(OXFORD UNIVERSITY PRESS)

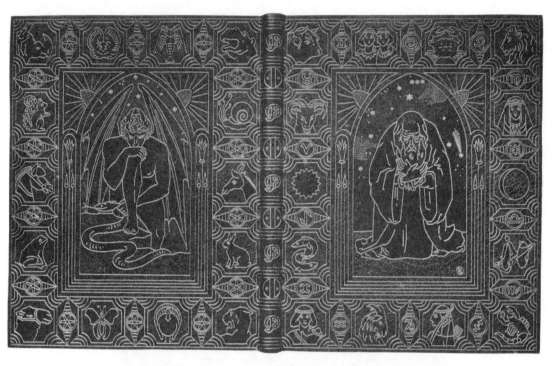

BOOKBINDING IN PURPLE LEVANT MOROCCO, WITH INLAY AND GOLD TOOLING. DESIGNED BY E. SPARKES
EXECUTED BY J. GREEN (OXFORD UNIVERSITY PRESS)

BOOKBINDING IN GREEN LEVANT MOROCCO, WITH INLAY AND GOLD TOOLING. DESIGNED BY J. GREEN
EXECUTED BY P. WARD (OXFORD UNIVERSITY PRESS)

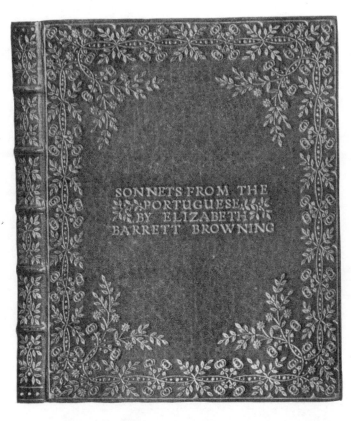

BOOKBINDING IN GREEN SEALSKIN, WITH INLAY AND GOLD TOOLING
BY MARY E. ROBINSON

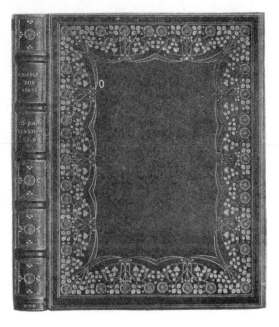

BOOKBINDING IN CRUSHED GREEN LEVANT MOROCCO
WITH GOLD TOOLING. BY ALICE PATTINSON (MRS.
RAYMUND ALLEN)

BOOKBINDING IN CRUSHED DARK BLUE LEVANT MOROCCO
WITH INLAY AND GOLD TOOLING. BY ALICE PATTINSON
(MRS. RAYMUND ALLEN)

97

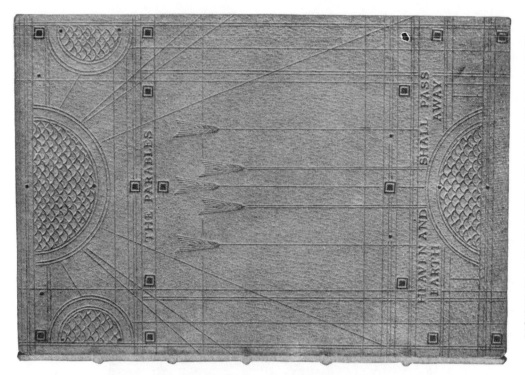

BOOKBINDING IN WHITE PIGSKIN, WITH BLIND AND GOLD TOOLING
BY SYBIL PYE

BOOKBINDING IN WHITE PIGSKIN, WITH BLIND AND GOLD TOOLING
BY SYBIL PYE

FLY-LEAF IN GREEN LEVANT MOROCCO, WITH POINTILLÉ AND INLAY
BY ROBERT RIVIERE AND SON

DOUBLURE IN LEVANT MOROCCO, WITH POINTILLÉ AND INLAY
BY ROBERT RIVIERE AND SON

DOUBLURE IN LEVANT MOROCCO, WITH INLAY
AND TOOLING. BY ROBERT RIVIERE AND SON.

Go thou to Rome,—at once the Paradise,
The grave, the city, and the wilderness;
And where its wrecks like shatter'd mountains rise,
And flowering weeds, and fragrant copses dress
The bones of Desolation's nakedness,
Pass, till the Spirit of the spot shall lead
Thy footsteps to a slope of green access,
Where, like an infant's smile, over the dead
A light of laughing flowers along the grass is spread.

The breath whose might I have invoked in song
Descends on me; my spirit's bark is driven,
Far from the shore, far from the trembling throng
Whose sails are never to the tempest given;
The massy earth and sphered skies are riven!
I am borne darkly, fearfully, afar;
Whilst, burning through the inmost veil of Heaven,
The soul of Adonais, like a star,
Beacons from the abode where the Eternal are.

SHELLEY

FLY LEAF IN GREEN LEVANT MOROCCO, WITH INLAY AND
GOLD TOOLING. BY F. SANGORSKI AND G. SUTCLIFFE

BOOKBINDING IN BLUE LEVANT MOROCCO, WITH GOLD TOOLING
BY F. SANGORSKI AND G. SUTCLIFFE

BOOKBINDING IN BLUE LEVANT MOROCCO, WITH GOLD TOOLING
BY F. SANGORSKI AND G. SUTCLIFFE

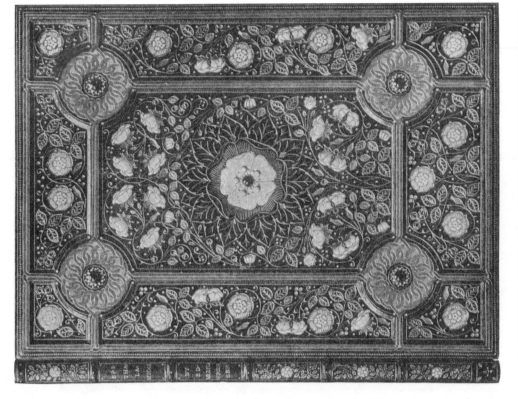

BOOKBINDING IN BROWN LEVANT MOROCCO, WITH INLAY AND GOLD TOOLING
BY F. SANGORSKI AND G. SUTCLIFFE

BOOKBINDING IN GREEN LEVANT MOROCCO, WITH INLAY AND GOLD TOOLING
BY F. SANGORSKI AND G. SUTCLIFFE

BOOKBINDING IN GREEN LEVANT MOROCCO, WITH GOLD TOOLING
BY F. SANGORSKI AND G. SUTCLIFFE

BOOKBINDING IN BLUE LEVANT MOROCCO, WITH INLAY AND GOLD TOOLING
BY F. SANGORSKI AND G. SUTCLIFFE

BOOKBINDING IN OLIVE MOROCCO, WITH GOLD TOOLING
CENTRE PANEL OF RED INLAY. BY A. DE SAUTY

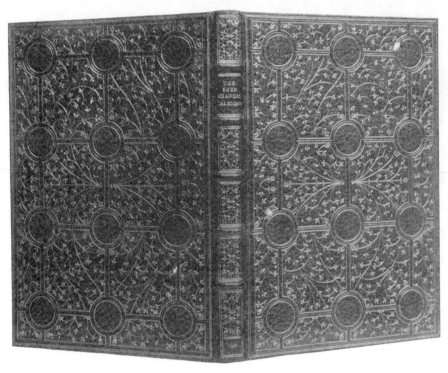

BOOKBINDING IN OLIVE MOROCCO, WITH GOLD TOOLING. BY A. DE SAUTY

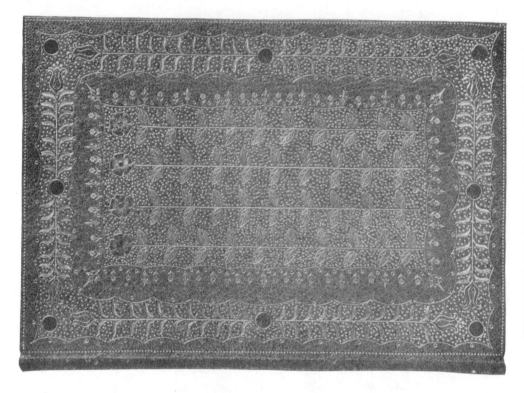

BOOKBINDING IN PINK MOROCCO, WITH INLAY AND GOLD TOOLING
BY SIR EDWARD SULLIVAN, BART.

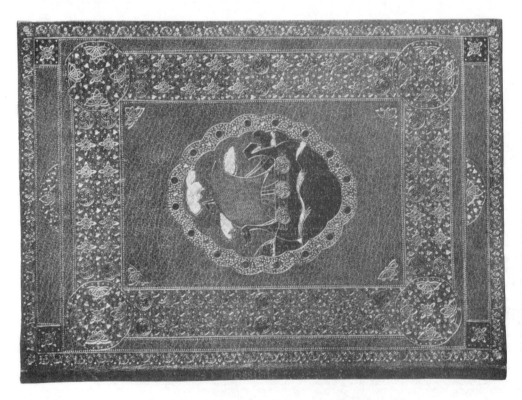

BOOKBINDING IN BLUE MOROCCO, WITH INLAY AND GOLD TOOLING
BY SIR EDWARD SULLIVAN, BART.

BOOKBINDING IN BLUE MOROCCO, WITH INLAY AND GOLD TOOLING. BY SIR EDWARD SULLIVAN, BART.

BOOKBINDING IN OLIVE GREEN LEVANT MOROCCO, WITH INLAY AND
GOLD TOOLING.   BY ZAEHNSDORF

BOOKBINDING IN YELLOW LEVANT MOROCCO, WITH INLAY AND
GOLD TOOLING.   BY ZAEHNSDORF

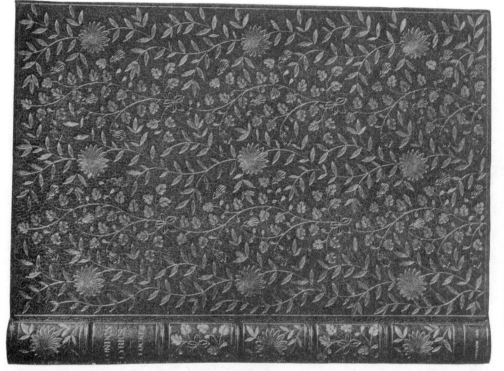

BOOKBINDING IN GREEN LEVANT MOROCCO, WITH INLAY AND
GOLD TOOLING. BY ZAEHNSDORF

BOOKBINDING IN BLUE LEVANT MOROCCO, WITH INLAY AND
GOLD TOOLING. BY ZAEHNSDORF

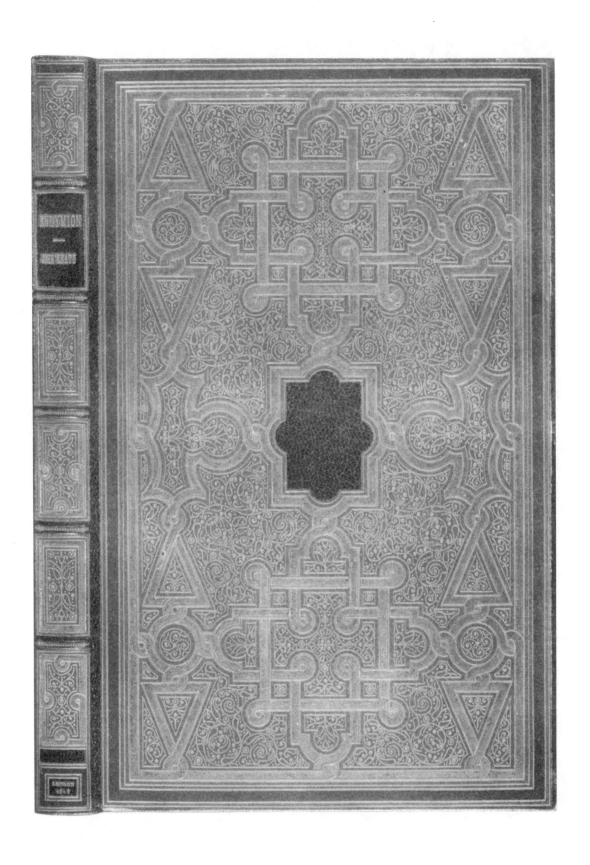

BOOKBINDING IN BLUE LEVANT MOROCCO, WITH
INLAY AND GOLD TOOLING. BY ZAEHNSDORF

BOOKBINDING IN BLUE LEVANT MOROCCO, WITH
INLAY AND GOLD TOOLING. BY ZAEHNSDORF

III

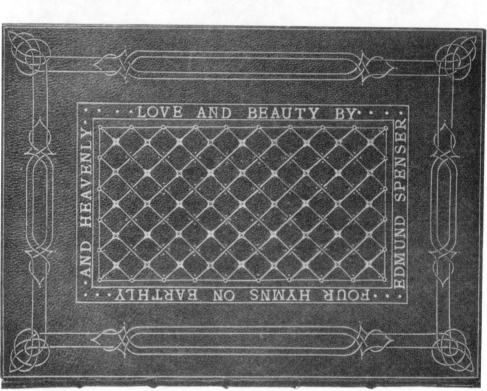

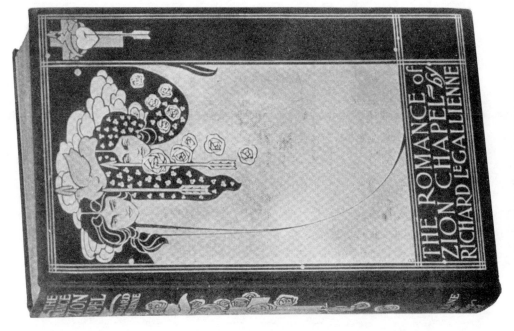

BINDING-CASE DESIGNED BY WILL BRADLEY
FOR MR. JOHN LANE

BINDING-CASE DESIGNED BY LAURENCE HOUSMAN
FOR MR. JOHN LANE

BINDING-CASE DESIGNED BY REGINALD L. KNOWLES
FOR MESSRS. J. M. DENT AND SONS LTD.

PICTURESQUE BRITTANY

By Mrs ARTHUR BELL
ILLUSTRATED BY
ARTHUR G BELL

PICTUR -ESQUE BRITT- ANY BY MRS ARTHUR BELL

ILLUST- RATED by ARTHUR G BELL

J. M DENT & CO

BINDING-CASE DESIGNED BY REGINALD L. KNOWLES
FOR MESSRS. J. M. DENT AND SONS LTD.

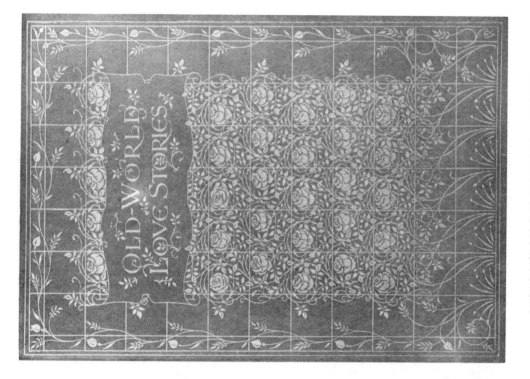

BINDING-CASE DESIGNED BY REGINALD L. KNOWLES
FOR MESSRS. J. M. DENT AND SONS LTD.

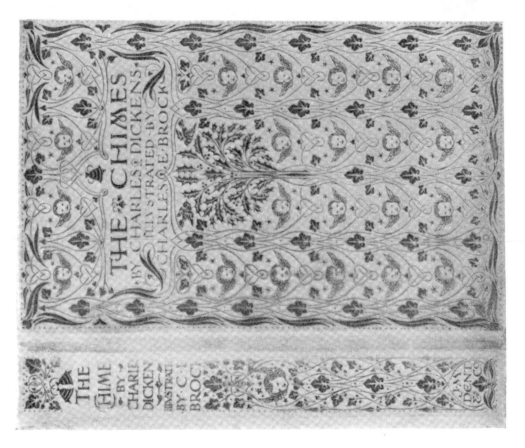

BINDING-CASE DESIGNED BY REGINALD L. KNOWLES
FOR MESSRS. J. M. DENT AND SONS LTD.

BINDING-CASE DESIGNED BY R. P. COSSOP
FOR MESSRS. J. M. DENT AND SONS LTD.

DESIGN FOR TITLE-PAGE OF "PAGAN PAPERS"
BY AUBREY BEARDSLEY

(By permission of Mr. John Lane)

DESIGN FOR COVER OF "THE WOMAN WHO DID"
BY AUBREY BEARDSLEY

118

DESIGN FOR COVER OF "NOBODY'S FAULT"
BY AUBREY BEARDSLEY

DESIGN FOR COVER OF "THE MOUNTAIN LOVERS"
BY AUBREY BEARDSLEY

(By permission of Mr. John Lane)

119

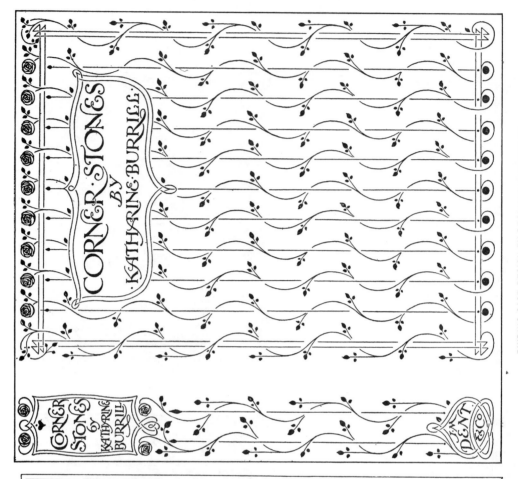

BINDING-CASE DESIGN BY REGINALD L. KNOWLES
FOR MESSRS. J. M. DENT AND SONS LTD.

BINDING-CASE DESIGN BY REGINALD L. KNOWLES
FOR MESSRS. J. M. DENT AND SONS LTD.

Inside design, in decorative banner:

EVERYMAN.
I·WILL·GO·WITH
·THEE
·&·BE·THY·GVIDE
·IN·THY·MOST·NEED
·TO·GO·BY·THY·SIDE

"THE HAUNT OF THE TROLL."—END-PAPER DESIGN BY REGINALD L. KNOWLES FOR "TALES FROM THE NORSE." PUBLISHED BY MESSRS. GEORGE ROUTLEDGE AND SONS, LTD.

END-PAPER DESIGN BY H. GRANVILLE FELL
FOR MESSRS. GEORGE NEWNES, LTD.

BORDER, INITIAL LETTERS, AND HEADPIECE DESIGNED
BY R. JAMES WILLIAMS. FOR THE VINCENT PRESS

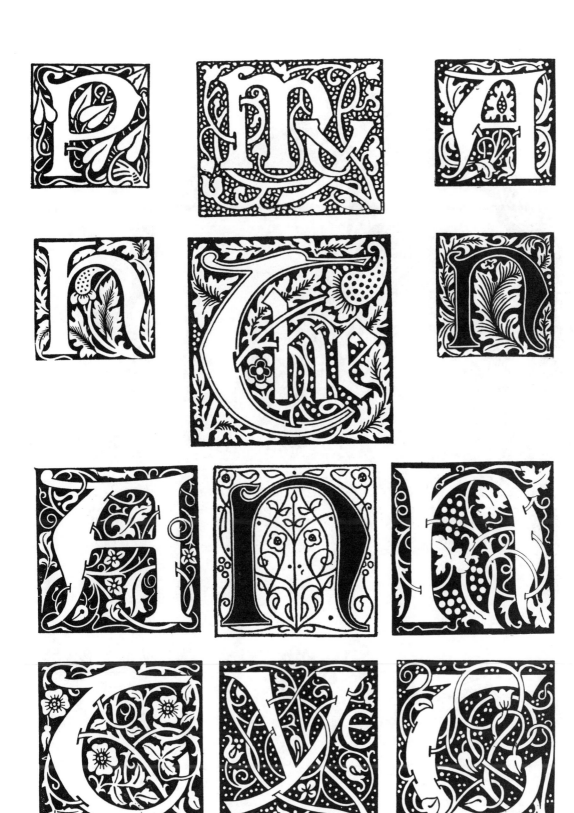

INITIAL LETTERS DESIGNED BY R. JAMES WILLIAMS. FOR THE VINCENT PRESS

"COÛTE QUIIL COÛTE"—DECORATIVE
DRAWING BY R. JAMES WILLIAMS

GERMANY

THE ART OF THE BOOK IN GERMANY. BY L. DEUBNER

"LETTERPRESS printing, even in the edition de luxe, is not an art, and neither the compositor nor the printer is an artist." This is what was written in the year 1887 by Ludwig Nieper, at that time Director of what is now the Royal Academy of the Graphic Arts and Book Industry at Leipzig, a city which in the present year has in its International Exhibition, embracing every conceivable aspect of the industry as well as the arts most closely bound up with it, furnished such a convincing and impressive demonstration of the culture uniting the nations as perhaps has never been offered before. The conviction expressed in the passage just quoted, repudiating the existence of any influence of art on industrial labour, belongs to a period bereft of any real feeling for art and content with the imitation and repetition of historic styles while eschewing any contact with the practical requirements of the industry. Nowadays we know how beneficial and fruitful for both has been the reciprocal influence of art and industry in every sphere of activity, and that only by this means have we been able to proceed from mere external embellishment to artistic form, from book adornment to a true art of the book. Thus in the space of barely twenty-five years our views of what art really is and what are its functions have radically changed, and it must be left to those who come after us to estimate more correctly than we are able to at the present day, the immense labour which has been accomplished in the space of a generation. The incipient stages in the growth of the new movement in Germany date back some twenty years. At that time we looked with envy at the publications which issued from the private presses of England, and could boast of nothing that could compare with the far-famed " Faust " of the Doves Press ; and if to-day we are at length able to stand on our own feet, it would yet be false to assert that the modern art of book production in Germany has developed from within, and to disavow the valuable stimulus and knowledge we owe especially to the English books of that period. And clearly as we perceived that the book in its entirety, with its harmonious co-ordination of type, decoration, composition, paper and binding, should form a work of art, yet only after many mistakes and deviations have we arrived at the goal. Thus nowadays no one would seriously seek to defend such a production as the official catalogue of the German section at the Paris Exhibition of 1900 ; and so, too, the so-called "Eckmann" type, which at one time was taken up with unexampled enthusiasm—a type in which the designer had contrived to adapt the ancient forms of the "Antiqua" type to the sinuous lines of modern ornament—is now almost completely forgotten. These and many other things which at that time were acclaimed as creative achievements, belong to that class of errors which are really nothing but exaggerated truths. But in the absence of such excesses and that exuberance of feeling which was so violently manifested, it would have been quite impossible to accomplish in so short a time what as a matter of fact was accomplished, and in spite of shortcomings has even now lost none of its importance in the history of the development of a new art of the book. ♔ The first event of significance which followed the renewed recognition of the decorative value of the printed letter was the issue of some new types designed by Otto Eckmann and Peter Behrens respectively, the former slender, delicate, and round, the latter bold, distinguished, and angular, but both alike quite free, natural, and easily legible. It was these founts that really inaugurated the new development; and the foundry of the Gebr. Klingspor which issued them, placed itself by so doing at the head of all those enterprising type-foundries which have since enriched our printing press with a wealth of new and valuable founts. It had come to be recognised that lettering and ornament were closely correlated; that the ornamentation of printed matter could not be regarded as an end in itself, but must be adapted to the character of the lettering in order that the rectangular space of a page should be so filled as to achieve a good general effect and satisfy the sensitive eye. Nothing remained, therefore, but to entrust the designing of new types to artists who had already accomplished good and original work as book decorators; and as none of the numerous German type-foundries desired or indeed could afford to be behindhand in a movement of this kind, it resulted that in the course of a few years the printing presses of the country were inundated with a flood of new "artist" types, of which, nevertheless, only relatively few have been able to survive till now. To design a new type or to re-mould the old forms of "Antiqua" (Roman) or "Fraktur" (German Gothic), so that the new forms should not only have a good black-and-white effect but that the eye should be able to grasp with ease the sequence of "word-pictures" as well as each individual letter and to read the lines quickly and comfortably, is a task of extraordinary difficulty which many who have attempted to grapple with have under-estimated. To obtain an idea of the multitude of difficulties that have to be overcome, one must bear in mind that the fundamental forms of the individual letters are fixed, and that only small changes are possible in the general shape, in the proportions of the component parts, in the alternation of the upright, horizontal, and oblique lines, in the curvature of the so-called "versal" or capital letters, in the serifs, and in the sweep of preliminary or terminal flourishes; that the printed letter, unlike manuscript, is bound up with fixed laws,

130

and that in order to justify its claim to consideration it should, while expressing the artistic individuality of its designer, not be too original and personal if it is to be employed for general use. Further, it should conform to the spirit and ideas of the age, and yet again it ought not to be wholly conditioned by contemporary considerations if it is to survive to a later age, as have many fine founts which the seventeenth and eighteenth centuries have bequeathed to us. ✠ As already said, only a few among our modern German designers of printed types have mastered all these difficulties, and among these few the names of Behrens, Tiemann, Koch, Kleukens, Weiss, and Wieynk are pre-eminent. In the course of some thirteen years that born architect, Peter Behrens, who began as a painter of easel pictures and a decorator of books, and now builds palaces, factory buildings, and gigantic business-houses, has himself designed four founts in which the whole artistic evolution of this strong-willed nature is reflected, and which yet seem so entirely the product of a natural growth that one is quite unconscious of the years of labour spent on their improvement and perfection in the interval between the preparation of the designs and the actual casting of the founts. As compared with the architectonic character of the austere, angular forms of the first Behrens type, the italic or "Kursiv" fount (p. 47) which made its appearance six years later looks more decorative with the gentle sweep and uniform flow of its lines, and in the most successful of the Roman founts the full vigour and monumentality of his later period of activity is clearly expressed ; while the most recent of all, the "Mediæval" (p. 46), which was only issued a few weeks ago, is again more ornamental with its uniformly fine lines, and admirably answers to its designation as a type embodying the characteristics of the Italian Renaissance script. ✠ Another "Mediæval" type which even excels that just mentioned in clearness and beauty of form has been designed by Walter Tiemann (pp. 146 and 147), who holds the position of instructor at the Royal Academy of Graphic Arts at Leipzig, and devotes himself almost exclusively to the improvement of the art of lettering and book production. Like all the other types designed by this artist, it has less of a personal character about it, and reason more than sentiment has been the guiding motive in the design ; but its cool, distinguished reticence gives it a quite exceptional merit. It is, moreover, completely independent of its classical prototypes and their Romanesque imitations ; very effective in all its gradations, the use of it is not restricted to the limited editions of our private presses, and in fact it is now one of the most popular founts we have. ✠ The fine Roman types by F. W. Kleukens (pp. 143, 144 and 153) rank among the most gratifying achievements of our new school. They are free from eccentricity of any kind, there is a seductive charm in their unassuming yet distinguished

131

forms, and even the ornamental slender kinds are agreeably clear. In spite of the thinness of their lines the letters belonging to this slender fount combine to make easily legible lines. The Kleukens types are practical as well as attractive, and in conjunction with specially designed borders, initials and decorative devices of all kinds, they are well adapted for the most diverse uses. ✠ Of a far more personal character, but at the same time of a more restricted range of use, are the graceful types by Heinrich Wieynk (pp. 149 and 150). It is the spirit of the Rococo that dwells therein—that epoch to which, with its playful charm and light-hearted grace, we owe so many masterpieces of French typography. Even the superfluous loops and flourishes which were characteristic of that period are encountered again, with many bizarre peculiarities, in the "Kursiv" and "Trianon" of Wieynk, and yet there is a remarkable fluidity and vitality in each stroke ; the general effect is highly artistic, and, as the examples now reproduced show, the founts are admirably adapted to numerous purposes. ✠ Many attempts have been made to modernise the old "Schwabacher" type, which dates from the middle of the fifteenth century, and differs from German Gothic, or "Fraktur," by being more compact. The most successful in this direction so far has been Rudolf Koch, whose "German Script," in the three different forms here shown (pp. 48, 140, 141 & 145), has once more revealed the rich beauty and massive power inherent in the various kinds of German type. In these boldly designed letters is expressed a manly earnestness and also a simple grandeur which, in the sweeping, powerful forms of the initials, becomes truly monumental. They are, moreover, carefully thought out in all their details, and notwithstanding the strength of the lines, even in the smallest sizes, they are very expressive in their beauty. ✠ Heinz König, too, has had good fortune with his "Schwabacher" type (p. 150). This is remarkably clear, and in its amalgamation of Roman forms with the characteristics of German founts it has proved both sound and serviceable, and it is one, moreover, which offers no difficulty whatever to the foreigner. The curls and loops which the champions of "Antiqua," or Roman, find fault with in the German styles of type are absent ; it is a Gothic purged of all unnecessary details and is at once dignified and decorative. ✠ Among the new "Fraktur" or German Gothic types mention should first of all be made of that known as "Weiss-Fraktur," which, designed by E. R. Weiss, has been perfected by him after many years of untiring collaboration with the Type Foundry of Bauer and Co. It has remained a purely German type, but is without the flourishes bequeathed by the old German Gothic. The light and open appearance of matter composed with it imparts to it a clarity which is distinctly agreeable, so that one can follow it with ease and comfort while deriving quiet pleasure from the simplicity and

132

definiteness of a type which satisfies in equal degree the requirements of use and æsthetic susceptibility. The Tempel Verlag, in common with a number of other important German publishing houses, has adopted the " Weiss-Fraktur" for its model editions of German classics. ⌘ When new desires call for satisfaction and new forms begin to develop, it is always those spheres of activity which offer easy and pleasant possibilities of accomplishment that are selected for experimenting. Thus some fifteen years ago the designing of bookbindings was a favourite occupation of the artists who interested themselves in the reform of industrial art, and many who have now attained to clear and definite ideas do not want to be reminded of the sort of work that was done in those days. Under the influence of Van de Velde's precept that every line is a force, the wrappers and bindings of books were among the things that were covered with a nervous labyrinth of lines which was expressive only of an attitude of mind radically at variance with all that had gone before. But many who at first occupied themselves with this kind of work in a more or less dilettante spirit, have by quiet, serious labour and steady development mastered its problems and have come to devote themselves almost exclusively to the graphic arts and the industry of book production, so that we now possess an important organisation of the workers in this field—the " Verein deutscher Buchgewerbekünstler"— whose collective exhibition at the International Exhibition now being held at Leipzig is one of the most interesting sections of this great display. Of the artists whose work is represented among the accompanying illustrations, Cissarz, Ehmcke, Kleukens, Köster, Koch, Renner, Steiner-Prag, Tiemann, Weiss and Wieynk belong to this group. ⌘ Johann Vincenz Cissarz had in 1900 already advanced to such prominence in this branch of work that the artistic arrangement of the German Typographical Section at the Paris Universal Exhibition was entrusted to him. A long way behind as this catalogue now is, it was nevertheless at that date an exemplary achievement as regards type, ornament, printing, and binding ; and to the large number of commissions it brought the artist may be due the fact that thereafter his chief attention was bestowed on the art of the book, in spite of his penchant and decided genius for painting of a decorative and even monumental character and his particular partiality for the etching-needle. From Dresden Cissarz migrated, first to Darmstadt and then to Stuttgart, where as teacher at the Royal School of Applied Art he found a welcome opportunity of communicating to others his own sound principles in regard to the internal and external arrangement of books, and already he is able to look back upon a teaching career which has been very successful. And here, too, many grateful tasks have fallen to him, not only in connection with special events, such as jubilees, presentation addresses, and such things, but

133

more especially in the course of work undertaken for the publishing houses of Stuttgart. Though the luxurious binding executed by hand in costly materials may be superior in an artistic sense, yet from the economic and cultural point of view the tastefully designed bindings produced in large quantities by the publishing houses are of greater importance. A series of these publishers' cases of diverse design is illustrated on pages 174 and 180, and it shows how successfully the designer has utilised the space to display his boldly lettered title or to cover the whole field with becoming ornament. ✠ Hugo Steiner-Prag, who first became known through his poetic drawings for children's fairy tales and books of verses, has also for some years past taught at the Royal Academy of Graphic Arts at Leipzig. His chief successes have been won as an illustrator, but from the bindings now reproduced (pp. 172 and 173) it will be seen that he has a marked talent for the embellishment of the book. By means of simple lines and decorative ornament, usually confined to a well-proportioned centre field, he achieves really charming effects. ✠ Karl Köster was at one time a pupil of Peter Behrens, and in order to be able to take advantage of all the possibilities open to the bookbinder he has not shrunk from learning the craft in the regular way. Thus in the course of his work he has not been wholly concerned with the external embellishment of the book, which he always endeavours to harmonise with its contents, but has also kept in view the practical purpose of the binding as a protective covering for the book. His great skill in achieving delightful effects with the simplest means is amply demonstrated by the numerous bindings he has designed for publishers. Thus in the bindings here illustrated, " Heimkehr " and " Buch Joram " (p. 175), three lines of lettering suffice to animate and decorate the entire surface ; but he is quite capable of employing much richer decorative devices with discretion and good taste. From the way in which he has placed a simple cross of violet leather in the richly ornamented middle field of his red missal binding (p. 169), to show to the greatest advantage the colour of the amethysts set in the silver mounts, it may be inferred that he is capable of producing new and peculiar arrangements of form and colour without breaking with the best traditions. In his second missal binding the form of the cross which dominates the entire space is distributed over twelve circular panels or fields, of which the middlemost is worked with a white leather inlay and gold-tooling. The other circles are lined with violet leather, and with the four amethysts of the corner rosettes, the sea-green morocco, and the rich gilding, produce a splendid effect of colour. ✠ Among the professional craftsmen who yielded to the new ideas of book production Paul Kersten is perhaps the best known, as he is without doubt the most successful. With an extensive practical experience, which has mastered all the

134

technical possibilities, he combines artistic susceptibility and a literary aptitude which has enabled him to uphold the objects he has at heart in thoughtfully written essays and books. As head of the Technical School for Bookbinders in Berlin he is in a position to exercise an educative influence in the best sense. The bindings illustrated on pages 170 and 171 enable one to judge of his technical versatility and his methods of decoration, which are not restricted to a particular scheme. They are without exception leather bindings in which the title is placed independently on the back or within a panel left for it, the ornamentation of the cover being therefore uninfluenced by it. In bindings of a richer character he is very fond of utilising a diversity of colours for the sake of the animating effect. Thus in his dark-blue morocco binding, whose centre panel is occupied by five hexagons within circles, the flowers displayed therein are of red, green, and violet leather ; while in the chamois binding of Baudelaire's "Fleurs du Mal," for the ornamentation of which, in gold and blind stamping, no fewer than 18,000 impressions were required, leather overlays in seven different colours were used. But even with such an abundance of decoration one is not conscious of any excess, but only perhaps that agreeable sense of assurance which the practised hand communicates. Three colours, black, red and blue, are employed for ornamenting the calf-binding with a circular centre panel, the decoration of which is carried out by a special process of tooling and staining. ✠ Of a much simpler character is the work of Franz Weisse, who likewise has come from the ranks of the handicraftsmen, and is now engaged as teacher at the School of Applied Art in Hamburg. The simple but bold stamping in which the decoration of his pigskin binding (p. 177) is executed comports well with the outspoken candour of Grimmelshausen's "Simplicissimus." A feature of interest is the use of the "batik" process * for producing floral ornament spread over the sides and back of the parchment binding. ✠ Again, in the richly decorated bindings of F. A. Demeter (pp. 167 and 168) one observes the sure hand of the experienced practitioner who knows how to take advantage of the beauties of material and technique in the fulfilment of his artistic aims. His ornamentation is certainly not quite original, but is distinguished by a clever decorative treatment of floral motives and a tasteful application of them ; and even when he completely covers the back and sides with decoration of a uniform character, one does not feel that it is overdone. A beautiful example of his work is the binding with a design of leafage in gold on a reseda-green leather. Demeter also is a professional binder, and

* Batik is a process of producing patterns by means of dyes and resists ; it has long been in use in the Dutch East Indies, whence it was introduced into Holland, and now has a considerable vogue both there and in Germany, Austria and Hungary.

135

at present is head of the applied art department of the Hübel and Denck wholesale bindery at Leipzig. Even these large industrial concerns, equipped for the wholesale production of cheap bindings, have been obliged to take account of the growing desire for books that have an artistic value, and to attach to their establishments special departments in which, under the supervision of artistically minded craftsmen, not only simple bindings in "boards," but also the costly and elaborate kinds of binding requiring most careful hand-work, are prepared. ❧ One of the most individual of the German artists who have devoted themselves to the modern art of the book is Emil Preetorius. He is a born illustrator, and has mastered all the various means of expression in equal degree; even in the very concise outline of the silhouette he achieves an abundance of characterisation and vitality. The silhouettes shown here (p. 165) are from a popular edition of Daudet's "Tartarin de Tarascon," which he has embellished and illustrated with refined artistic feeling; they figure there merely as the decorative headpieces to certain of the chapters, and serve as a jocose premonition of what is to follow. They are not the actual illustrations of the book, but they certainly afford an excellent idea of the happy way in which with these queer little black figures he has caught the grotesque comicality of this strange adventure. He is also fond of giving the reader in his title-pages a foretaste of what awaits him, of expressing graphically, in drawings often containing a number of figures, the contents and spirit of the books in which they appear. His figures are mostly those of people who lived in the "Biedermeier" age; they have a distinctly old-fashioned look about them, but none of that sentimental "gush" which so often makes the so-called "Stimmung" pictures of that period unpalatable to us moderns. While having a decided partiality for the peculiarities and foibles of the "Biedermeier" folk, Preetorius is thoroughly modern in feeling; his drawings are austere rather than sweetly sentimental, and even their æsthetic defects are pertinent to his art. ❧ The part played by various enterprising and ideally minded publishing houses in fostering and stimulating that pleasure in beautiful books and their acquisition which has increased to such an extraordinary degree in Germany during the past decade must not go unrecorded here. Among these the firm of Eugen Diederichs, of Jena, claims primary consideration because of the ungrudging spirit in which it has afforded to all who have made a name in the sphere of artistic book-production an opportunity of displaying their ideas and skill. This firm caters for all the manifold cultural tendencies of our age, and its publications being of a serious character, the collaboration of these artists has been in the main restricted to wrappers and bindings, title-pages, initials, ornamental borders, and other decorative details. On the other hand, there are houses, such as that of Georg Müller in Munich, which besides good decoration go in largely for book illustration, in which also numerous and interesting developments have taken place, including a revival of various processes—such as wood-engraving, lithography, and etching—that had fallen largely into disuse, but now once more enjoy considerable favour for the purpose of book illustration. The Insel-Verlag of Leipzig, S. Fischer of Berlin, Paul and Bruno Cassirer of Berlin, Kurt Wolff of Leipzig, and many others, have helped materially in this reflorescence of German illustrative art. But at the same time, there are more than a few who hold that a well-printed book with unimpeachable letterpress, paper and binding requires neither decoration nor illustration, and that its intrinsic merit depends on the perfect manner in which the technical work is carried out. Thus the celebrated editions of the Hyperion Press and the splendid issues of the Century Press of the Munich publishing firm of Hans von Weber are brilliant examples of German typography; nor need the publications of the Janus Press of Leipzig, produced with consummate technical care under the supervision of Walter Tiemann and Carl Ernst Poeschel, fear comparison with the books that issue from the private presses of England. These volumes are only printed in small editions of one hundred and fifty to two hundred copies, and satisfy the utmost demands of discriminating bibliophiles. Of distinction on account of their typically German character are the " Rudolfinische Drucke," brought out by Rudolf Koch in association with Rudolf Gerstung at Offenbach, and published by Wilhelm Gerstung. In these books, which are also genuinely German in their contents, everything is expressly avoided which in any way deviates from the considerations of chief importance—proper spacing of the letters and the well-balanced composition of the page of letterpress in Koch's essentially German fount,

TITLE-PAGE DESIGNED BY PROF. PAUL LANG-KURZ

together with uniform excellence of workmanship throughout. Thus only the title-pages are specially designed, and the body of the letterpress is but sparingly relieved with the imposing initials belonging to this fount ; but the bindings, with their cover-papers cut and printed by the artist himself, also bear witness to the virile beauty of his art. Of a more arresting and luxurious character are the productions of the Ernst Ludwig Press of the Grand Duke of Hesse, the artistic supervision of which has been entrusted to F. W. Kleukens ; and the costly editions de luxe of the Pan-Press of Berlin, which are emebllished with lithographs by Slevogt, Corinth and Pascin, or etchings by Geiger or Walser. Such productions, however, are beyond the scope of this work. ✠ What Germany is now able to offer in the art of book production is superabundantly shown in the International Exhibition which is being held this year at Leipzig. That after barely a score of years we should have seriously ventured to invite the civilised races to peaceful competition in this special domain is a proof that we are conscious of the value of our work, and do not fear the verdict of the world.

ORNAMENT DESIGNED BY
PROF. F. W. KLEUKENS, FOR
D. STEMPEL, FRANKFURT A.M.

Im künstlerhaus findet
vom 25·April bis 30·Mai
eine Ausstellung buchge=
werblicher Arbeiten von
hans Wehrle·Straßburg
statt·Ausgestellt werden
Bücher·Diplome·Plakate
und anderes

A GERMAN TYPE DESIGNED BY RUDOLF KOCH
CAST BY GEBR. KLINGSPOR, OFFENBACH A.M.

Juli

Klingt im Wind ein Wiegenlied,
Sonne warm hernniederseht,
Seine Ähren senkt das Korn,
Rote Beere schwillt am Dorn,
Schwer von Segen ist die Flur -
Junge Frau, was sinnst du nur?

Mondlicht

Wie liegt im Mondenlichte
Begraben nun die Welt;
Wie selig ist der Friede,
Der sie umpfangen hält.

Die Winde müssen schweigen,
So sanft ist dieser Schein;
Sie säuseln nur und weben
Und schlafen endlich ein.

Und was in Tagesgluten
Zur Blüte nicht erwacht,
Es öffnet seine Kelche
Und duftet in der Nacht.

Wie bin ich solchen Friedens
Seit lange nicht gewohnt!
Sei du in meinem Leben
Der liebevolle Mond!

Gedichte
von Theodor Storm

Verlag: Gebr. Paetel·Berlin

A GERMAN TYPE DESIGNED BY RUDOLF KOCH
CAST BY GEBR. KLINGSPOR, OFFENBACH A.M.

Eine preußische
Königstochter

Denkwürdigkeiten der Markgräfin
von Bayreuth

Schwester Friedrichs des Großen

Herausgegeben von Johannes Armbruster

Mit einem Bildnis der Markgräfin

Wilhelm Langewiesche-Brandt
Ebenhausen bei München

THE "WIEYNK-KURSIV" TYPE, DESIGNED BY HEINRICH WIEYNK
CAST BY THE BAUERSCHE GIESSEREI, FRANKFURT A.M.

VOLKSKUNST UND VOLKSGUNST

NUR der Kundige weiß es, daß die schönen Erzeugnisse der bäuerlichen Handfertigkeit so ziemlich
aufgekauft sind. Die Landbewohner entledigten
sich mit Freuden des alten Plunders, um dafür
die ihrer Meinung nach vornehmere städtische
Fabrikware in buntestem Durcheinander anzuschaffen. Der
Sucht, es den Städtern gleich zu tun, konnte auch die treueste
Anhänglichkeit an sehr wertvolle alte Erbstücke nicht wider-
stehen. So erleben wir die merkwürdige Tatsache, bäuerische
Dielen mit all den schönen Gegenständen in einfachster
Künstlerschaft in städtischen Wohnräumen wiederzufinden
und die Häuser der Landbewohner im ödesten Geschmack
protziger Kleinstädter ausgestattet zu sehen. Alles dreht sich!
Der Vorgang ist ein natürlicher. Seit der Zeit, da es auf
dem Lande als selbstverständlich gilt, jeden zur Verfügung
stehenden Wohnraum für klingendes Geld an städtische
Sommergäste zu vermieten, mußten die alten und schönen
Erzeugnisse bäuerischer Künstler auf Geschmacksmenschen
der Städte einen sehr großen Einfluß ausüben. Daraus ist
die Wechselwirkung entstanden. Gewiß ist es heute noch
möglich, hier und dort in verlorenen Winkeln eine schöne
bemalte Truhe, einen schweren geschnitzten Schrank, sowie
zinnerne Becher, Teller, Leuchter, ja sogar noch Porzellan
zu entdecken, aber wer wirklich Volkskunst finden will, der
wird in die Museen gehen müssen, die gottlob vor den
Spüraugen englischer Sammler noch vieles gerettet haben.
Wir können ruhig sagen, daß der künstlerische Betätigungs-
drang im Volke noch nicht verloren gegangen ist; aber er
ist verwirrt, verstümmelt und verdorben. Die Geschmacks-
verheerungen der verflossenen Stilrevolution spuken in den
Städten noch herum, es ist also nur ein natürlicher Vorgang,
wenn wir ihnen jetzt auch auf dem Lande überall begegnen.
Die beste Ueberlieferung kann allmählich verloren gehen.
Setzte sich irgend ein großstädtischer Protz in einem Dorfe
fest, so genügte seine Bau- und Lebensweise vollkommen,
um die ganze Gegend nach und nach künstlerisch zu veröden.

32

THE "SCHLANKE KLEUKENS-ANTIQUA" TYPE. DESIGNED BY PROF. F. W.
KLEUKENS, CAST BY THE BAUERSCHE GIESSEREI, FRANKFURT A.M.

seines Innern, seiner Seele. Wird das Ausstellungsmaterial, von diesem Standpunkt vereinigt geordnet und bewertet, wird dieser Gesichtspunkt auch dem ganzen Unternehmen gegenüber von der Leitung zur Geltung gebracht, dann schildert jede verständnisvoll ausgebaute Abteilung Natur und Seele in inniger Verknüpfung und Wechselwirkung. So erhebt sich das in Leipzig geplante Werk nicht allein zum Sammelpunkt alles dessen, was bisher erreicht ist, sondern zur ungeheueren ideell belebenden Kraft für den einheitlichen Vormarsch unserer Technik und Kultur!

DIE KINEMATOGRAPHIE AUF DER BUCHGEWERBEAUSSTELLUNG IN LEIPZIG

Geradezu beispiellos ist die Entwicklung der Kinematographie gewesen. Der armselige flimmernde Kinematograph um 1900, der wie eine krankhafte Spielerei von kleinen Unternehmern den kleinen Leuten in fragwürdigen Buden und schlechten niedrigen Läden vorgeführt wurde, ist nicht mehr. Der Typus jenes Kinematographen von ehedem, der brutal, schreiend bunt wie seine Plakate, auf die verworrenen Sinne des niederen Volkes spekulierte, liegt in den letzten Zügen. Der Kinematograph von heute bannt sein Publikum, das nicht mehr zu unterscheiden ist von dem des Sprech-Theaters, in großen, wundervollen Lichtspielhäusern mit der Gebärde und dem mimischen Spiel der größten Schauspieler, er rollt mit unbeschreiblich lebenswahrem Ausdruck die Wogen des Meeres über den Strand und läßt das Laub der Silberpappel leise im Winde zittern, er zeigt mit einer Klarheit, die etwas Schreckliches hat, den Kampf der Blutkörper mit den Spirochaeten des Fiebers und läßt alle die komplizierten Maschinen, die der Mensch erfunden, lautlos vor uns ihre Arbeit verrichten. Das Wesen des Kinematographen ist nicht mehr ohne Würde, nicht mehr ohne Form und Inhalt. Wer steht nicht alles im Dienste des Filmbildes! Zuerst waren es die Bühnenkünstler, auch die Größen kamen; dann die Maler und Wissenschaftler und zuletzt – ein wenig widerstrebend zwar – die Literaten. Einmal haben dem Kinematographen die bedeutenden Verbesserungen geholfen, mit der die Aufnahme- und die Wiedergabeapparate ausgestattet wurden, auch die Verwendung des Mikroskopes und

Sechstes Kapitel 1505-08

Giulio der Zweite ~ Giuliano di San Gallo, Berufung nach Rom, Bramante ~ Grabmonument des Papftes ~ Umgeftaltung der alten Bafilika von St. Peter ~ Reife nach Carrara ~ Sinnesänderung des Papftes ~ Flucht ~ Schreiben Giulio's an die Signorie von Florenz ~ Anerbieten von feiten des Sultans ~ Rückkehr nach Rom als Gefandter der Republik ~ Feldzug des Papftes gegen Bologna ~ Einnahme der Stadt

Die Politik des Vatikans hatte durch den Wechfel der Perfonen keine allzugroße Veränderung erlitten. Cefare Borgia's Zweck war die Herftellung eines nationalen einigen Reiches gewefen, Giulio der Zweite wollte nichts Anderes. Auch er hatte eine Familie, die er groß zu machen fuchte, auch ihn unterftützten Gift, Mord, Verftellung und offene Gewaltfamkeit. Wie die Borgia's mußte er zwifchen Spanien und Frankreich die vorteilhaftefte Mitte zu halten fuchen. In zwei Punkten aber unterfchied er fich vom Papfte Alexander: er ließ nicht durch Andere Krieg führen, fondern zog in eigener Perfon zu Felde und was er eroberte, follte der Kirche gehören und nicht den Rovere's, feiner Familie. Diefe befchränkte er auf Urbino, ihr Herzogtum. Als er ftarb, hinterließ er einen Schatz in den Gewölben der Engelsburg, den feine Verwandten nicht berühren durften, den kein anderer als der auf ihn folgende Papft befitzen follte. Eine rauhe, ftolze Würde liegt in Giulios Auftreten und feine Wildheit artete nie in Graufamkeit aus. Was ihn aber vor allen anderen Päpften vor ihm und nach ihm geadelt hat, ift feine Freude an den Werken großer Künftler und der Blick, mit dem er fie erkannte und zu fich emporzog.

Unter den Männern, die er fogleich nach Rom berief, war einer der vornehmften Giuliano di San Gallo. Diefer hatte in früheren Zeiten Oftia für ihn, als Kardinal Vincula, befeftigt. Man fetzt diefe Bauten in den Anfang der achtziger Jahre. Sangallo kam, als er damals nach Oftia berufen ward, aus Neapel, wo er im Auftrage des alten Lorenzo dei Medici einen Palaft für den Herzog von Calabrien, den Sohn des Königs, baute. Er gehörte zu den glücklichen Leuten, die überall Ruhm und fürftliches Wohlwollen finden. In Mailand war er von Ludovico Sforza glänzend empfangen worden; in Rom mußte er für Vincula einen Palaft bauen, Alexander VI. befchäftigte ihn. Cefare Borgia desgleichen; in Savona, dem Geburtsort der Rovere, baute er für Vincula wiederum, dem er dann nach Frankreich folgte, wo ihn der König in Affection nahm; endlich, nach Florenz zurückgekehrt, wurde er von der Regierung mit fortlaufenden Arbeiten verfehen, bis ihn jetzt fein alter Gönner abermals nach Rom befahl. Sangallo machte den Papft auf Michelangelo aufmerkfam, und mitten aus der Arbeit am Karton heraus wurde diefer jetzt nach Rom berufen. Hundert Scudi Reifegeld zahlte man ihm auf der Stelle aus. Er muß zu Anfang des Jahres 1505 in Rom eingetroffen fein.

Giulio wußte, trotz der Eile, mit der er ihn verlangt hatte, nicht gleich, was er ihm zu tun geben follte. Einige Zeit ging darüber hin, bis er ihm den Auftrag zu einem koloffalen Grabmonumente erteilte, das er für fich felber im Sankt Peter errichten laffen wollte. Michelangelo entwarf eine Zeichnung und der Papft, entzückt davon, befahl ihm, in der Bafilika von Sankt Peter fogleich den beften Platz für das Monument ausfindig zu machen. Diefe Kirche, ein ungeheures Werk aus den älteften Zeiten des Chriftentums, an dem Jahrhunderte hindurch weitergebaut worden war, befaß eine Fülle von Kunftfchätzen. Giotto

75

A GERMAN TYPE DESIGNED BY RUDOLF KOCH
CAST BY GEBR. KLINGSPOR, OFFENBACH A.M.

FRANÇOIS MONTCORBIER wurde 1431 zu Paris als der Sohn armer Eltern aus der niedrigsten Volksschichte geboren. Den Namen Villon nahm er von seinem «plus que père» Guillaume de Villon, einem Kaplan der Kirche St. Benoît le Bétourné zu Paris, an, der sich um seine jedenfalls arg vernachlässigte Erziehung kümmerte und ihn zu sich nahm. Er ermöglichte François auch den Besuch der Schule der Faculté des Arts, wo derselbe Latein, Logik und Rhetorik lernte. Später, aber nicht lang verdiente er seinen Lebensunterhalt als Schreiber bei einem Juristen. Der junge Bursche, der schon als kleiner Knabe jedenfalls in dem armen Viertel, wo seine Eltern wohnten, auf der Gasse so manches sah, was nicht gerade nach Moral roch, geriet leicht auf Abwege. Als armer Student, der wie seine Gefährten sein Brot durch Betteln verdiente, in elenden Quartieren hauste, dabei der Freund von Dirnen und Zuhältern war, führte er ein rechtes Lotterleben und zog bald die Aufmerksamkeit der Behörden auf sich. Heute

FRANÇOIS VILLON

DES MEISTERS WERKE
INS DEUTSCHE ÜBERTRAGEN
VON K·L·AMMER

LEIPZIG
VERLAG VON JULIUS ZEITLER

THE "MEDIÆVAL" TYPE. DESIGNED BY PROF. WALTER TIEMANN, CAST BY GEBR. KLINGSPOR, OFFENBACH A.M.

ON PROPRIETY

IN THE RIGHT GOVERNMENT OF A STATE the rules of propriety serve the same purpose as the steel= yard in determining what is light and what is heavy; or, as the carpenter's line in determining what is square and what is round. If the weights of the steelyard be true, there can be no imposition in the matter of weight; if the line be rightly applied there will be no doubt about the evenness of the sur= face; if the square and compass be exact there will be no uncertainty as to the shape of the figure. When a superior man conducts the government of his State with a discrimin= ating attention to these rules of propriety he cannot be imposed on by traitors and impostors. The ceremonies of the Court audiences at the different seasons were intended to illustrate the righteous relations between ruler and subject; the friendly messages and inquiries to illustrate the mutual honor and respect between the feudal princes; those of mourning and sacrifice, to illustrate the kindly feelings of ministers and sons; those of social meetings in the country district, to show the order that should prevail between young and old; and those of marriage to exhibit the separation that should be maintained between males and females. Those ceremonies prevent the rise of disorder and confusion, and are like embankments which prevent the overflow of water. He who thinks the old em= bankments useless and destroys them is sure to suffer from the desolation caused by the overflowing water; and he who considers the old rules of propriety useless and would abolish them, would be sure to suffer from the calamities of disorder. If the ceremonies of marriage were discontinued, the path or husband and wife would be embittered, and there would be many instances of licentiousness and depravity. If the drinking ceremonies at country feasts were discontinued, the order bet= ween old and young would be neglected, and quarrelsome liti= gations would be frequent. If the ceremonies of mourning and sacrifice were omitted the kindly feeling of officers and sons

THE "MEDIÆVAL" TYPE. DESIGNED BY PROF. WALTER
TIEMANN, CAST BY GEBR. KLINGSPOR, OFFENBACH A.M.

HANS VON MARÉES
AUSSTELLUNG VON WERKEN
IN DEN SÄLEN DES
FRANKFURTER KUNSTVEREINS

AUS DER LEBENSGESCHICHTE VON
HANS VON MARÉES

Über die Abstammung Hans von Marées' sind manche Irrtümer verbreitet. Er wird mit Unrecht für den Abkömmling französischer Emigranten gehalten. Die uralte Familie – viel älter als die Emigration –, die u. a. auch in Frankreich verbreitet ist, stammt aus Flandern. Seit dem 16. Jahrhundert ist der deutsche Zweig am Rhein ansässig. Ein Ahne unseres Künstlers, geborener Bremer, geht nach Schweden und heiratet eine Schwedin. Einer ihrer Söhne ist der bayrische Hofmaler des 18. Jahrhunderts, Georg de Marées, dessen Bildnisse im Schleißheimer Schlosse und in anderen, namentlich bayrischen Sammlungen hängen. Hans von Marées ist nicht sein Nachkomme, sondern der Urenkel eines anderen Sohnes der Schwedin. Dieser ging als Prediger nach Dessau zu Leopold von Anhalt. Dort blieb die Familie bis zum Vater des Malers. Die meisten Marées waren Pastore und oft nicht nur des geistlichen, auch des gereimten weltlichen Wortes mächtig. Die Dichtergabe ist am stärksten in Adolf von Marées, dem Vater von Hans, ausgebildet. Adolf von Marées war ein hervorragender Jurist. Er heiratete 1830 als dreißigjähriger die Tochter des Bankiers Sußmann in Halberstadt, eine Jüdin von reicher Bildung des Herzens und des Geistes. Das Paar lebte zuerst in Düsseldorf, dann in Elberfeld überaus glücklich, nicht ohne Wohlstand, und allen edlen Interessen, zumal der Literatur, eifrig ergeben. Dies die Eltern. Hans von Marées wurde in Elberfeld am 24. Dezember 1837 geboren. 1847 siedelte die Familie nach Coblenz über, wo der Vater Präsident des Kammergerichts wurde. Hier verlebte Hans die glücklichste Kindheit. Er sollte ursprünglich wie seine Brüder Offizier werden. Mit einer auffallenden Bestimmtheit entschied er sich schon früh für den Malerberuf. Beleg seines Talentes waren die Porträtzeichnungen nach den Freunden des Hauses, die schon um das Jahr fünfzig beginnen. Die Mutter, zu der er sich, so lange sie lebte, am meisten hingezogen fühlte, unterstützte den Wunsch. Nicht ohne Widerstreben gab der

THE "MEDIÆVAL-KURSIV" TYPE. DESIGNED BY PROF. WALTER TIEMANN, CAST BY GEBR. KLINGSPOR, OFFENBACH A.M.

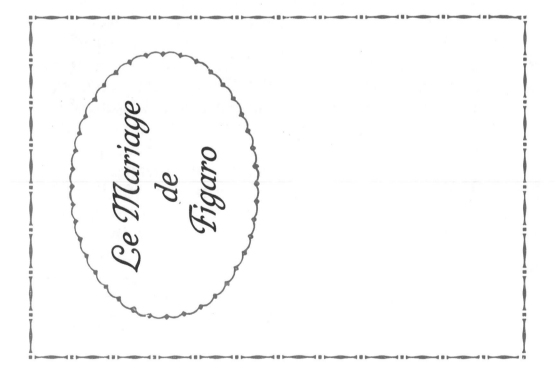

Le Mariage de Figaro

Acte premier

Le théâtre représente une chambre à demi-démeu-blée, un grand fauteuil de malade est au milieu. Figaro avec une toise me-sure le plancher. Suzanne attache à sa tête, devant une glace, le petit bouquet de fleur d'orange, appellé Chapeau de la Mariée.

Scène première

Figaro, Suzanne

Figaro Dix-neuf pieds sur vingt six.

Suzanne Tiens, Figaro, voilà mon petit cha-peau: le trouves-tu mieux-ainsi?

Figaro lui prends les mains Sans comparaison ma charmante. O! que ce joli bouquet virginal, élevé sur la tête d'une belle fille, est doux, le matin de noce, à l'œil amoureux d'un époux!....

Suzanne se retire Que mesures-tu donc là, mon fils?

Figaro Je regarde, ma petite Suzanne, si ce beau lit que Monseigneur nous donne, aura bonne grace ici.

THE "TRIANON" TYPE. DESIGNED BY HEINRICH WIEYNK CAST BY THE BAUERSCHE GIESSEREI, FRANKFURT A.M.

Frühjahrs=Katalog

Am Beginn der Frühjahrs=Saison beehre ich mich ergebenst, Ihnen meinen Katalog mit der Bitte zu überreichen, denselben einer gefälligen Durchsicht zu unterziehen und bei Besorgung der Einkäufe geneigtest berücksichtigen zu wollen. Ferner erlaube ich mir, Ihnen anzuzeigen, daß sämtliche Neuheiten in deutschen und englischen Stoffen für die Frühjahrs= und Sommer=Saison am Lager sind und gebe ich auf den nachfolgenden Blättern einen kleinen Überblick über die maßgebendsten Modelle. Die Anfertigung feiner Damen= und herren=Moden erfolgt in eigener Maßschneiderei unter Garantie tadelloser Ausführung zu mäßigen Preisen. Außerdem gestatte ich mir, auf mein Lager fertiger Damen= und herren=Garderoben hinzuweisen, das reichhaltige Auswahl in modernen Kleidungsstücken bietet und den verwöhntesten Anforderungen entspricht. Als Spezialität führe ich ein großes Lager sämtlicher Sport=Bekleidungen für Rasen= und Wassersport sowie für Touristik. Durch meine jahrelangen Erfahrungen ist es mir möglich, meinen Kunden mit sachgemäßen Ratschlägen dienen und nur Vorzügliches bieten zu können, und hoffe ich, mit Ihren geschätzten Aufträgen beehrt zu werden.

THE "SCHWABACHER" TYPE. DESIGNED BY HEINZ
KÖNIG, CAST BY EMIL GURSCH, BERLIN

SONETTO

DI ANTONIO PUCCI SOVRA IL RITRATTO DI DANTE

Questo che veste di color sanguigno,
posto seguente alle merite sante,
dipinse Giotto in figura di Dante,
che di parole fe' sì bell'ordigno.

E come par nell'abito benigno,
così nel mondo fu, con tutte quante
quelle virtù, ch'onoran chi davante
le porta con affetto nello scrigno.

Diritto paragon fu di sentenze:
col braccio manco avvinchia la scrit=
perchè signoreggiò molto scïenze. (tura

E 'l suo parlar fu con tanta misura,
che 'ncoronò la città di Firenze
di pregio, onde ancor fama le dura.

Perfetto di fattezze è qui dipinto,
com'a sua vita fu di carne cinto.

THE "HÖLZL-MEDIÆVAL" TYPE. DESIGNED BY EMIL
HÖLZL. CAST BY D. STEMPEL, FRANKFURT A·M.

WER BUECHER LIEST,
VERDIENT DEN PREIS
VOR EINEM, DER UN=
WISSEND IST, UND DER
IST JENEM VORZUZIE=
HEN, DER DAS GELESE=
NE NICHT VERGISST;
EIN SOLCHER IST VON
HOEHERM WERT, DER
DAS GELESENE AUCH
VERSTEHT, DOCH HOE=
HEREN WERT ALS DIE
SER HAT DER MANN,
DER DANACH FRISCH
ANS HANDELN GEHT

INDISCHER SPRUCH

THE "HÖLZL-MEDIÆVAL" TYPE. DESIGNED BY EMIL
HÖLZL, CAST BY D. STEMPEL, FRANKFURT A.M.

ZIELE UND AUSSICHTEN DER GARTENSTADT-BEWEGUNG

VON
DR. KARL MANGOLD
DRESDEN

AS Problem des Städtebaues ist heute, im Gegensaß zu früher, wo unsere Städte klein und ihr Wachstum gering war, bei dem ungeheueren Wachstum derselben außerordentlich dringlich. Die schwersten Mißstände liegen vor: die große Masse der Bevölkerung ist von der Natur in einem Grade abgeschlossen, wie er in der deutschen Geschichte überhaupt noch nicht dagewesen ist; die ganze Anlage der Städte ist nicht entfernt so planvoll, wie sie sein müßte. Die Preise des Bodens sowie der Wohnungen sind ungeheuerlich und vor allem auch der äußere Anblick von einer schreckenerregenden Häßlichkeit. Wohl hat man durch Bauordnungen und Bebauungspläne, durch Schaffung öffentlicher Anlagen, durch Anlegen von Villenstadtteilen und Vororten und ähnliches mehr Abhilfe zu schaffen versucht, aber doch nur mit ganz ungenügendem Erfolge.

Es drängt sich der Gedanke auf zu versuchen, auf einer neuen Grundlage, auf billigem Land draußen, ganz neue Städte aufzubauen, die nicht durch die Sünden der Vergangenheit belastet sind. Vorstufen zu einem solchen Vorgehen sind ja ohnedies vorhanden in den Gründungen so mancher großen Terrain-Gesellschaften, namentlich in Berlin und Umgebung, ferner in den großen Arbeiter-Kolonien der Großindustrie, wie z. B. in den bekannten Anlagen der Firma Krupp, und endlich auch in einigen ganz besonders hervorragenden und umfangreichen Baugenossenschafts-Gründungen. Hier reiht sich nun zwanglos der Gedanke der Gartenstadt ein, der aus England zu uns gekommen ist. Dort veröffentlichte Ende 1898 Ebenezer Howard, von Beruf Stenograph und jeßt am Ende der fünfziger Jahre stehend, ein Buch 'To morrow' (später unter dem Titel 'Garden Cities of to morrow', deutsch unter dem Titel 'Gartenstädte in Sicht', Jena, Diederichs), das großes Aufsehen erregte. Es geht aus von dem Grundgedanken, daß auf der einen Seite die großen Städte überfüllt, auf der anderen das Land entvölkert sei und daß es darauf ankomme, Stadt und Land miteinander zu vermählen durch Schaffung von Gartenstädten, welche die Vorteile des Landes mit denen der Stadt vereinigen. Eine solche Gartenstadt soll nur eine begrenzte Größe haben, etwa 30000 Einwohner, dann soll ein dauernd zu erhaltender, großer landwirt-

THE "INGEBORG-ANTIQUA" TYPE. DESIGNED BY PROFESSOR
F. W. KLEUKENS, CAST BY D. STEMPEL, FRANKFURT A.M.

Villiers de l'Isle-Adam

Le Nouveau Monde

orné de 15 bois originaux
en 2 couleurs de P.E.Vibert

GEORGES CRÈS et Cie
116, Bd St GERMAIN
Paris
1913

GIROUETTES

LES hommes sages comparent volontiers leurs contemporains à des girouettes que le moindre vent fait virer. Moi qui suis l'ami des girouettes, je pense qu'on a peut-être tort de les juger si légèrement. Lorsque dans l'espoir, souvent déçu, de voir le ciel s'éclaircir, je lève les yeux vers le petit peuple girouettique, je vois le laboureur se diriger exactement vers l'endroit que vise le chasseur, et le bateau voguer dans la même direction, et le lévrier courir au même but, et la sirène indiquer du doigt le même point mystérieux. Il y a donc entente absolue entre toutes les girouettes. Aimer le changement ne me paraît pas si détestable que ça.... L'important c'est que tout le monde soit d'accord.

George Auriol.

PAGE PRINTED IN ITALIC FACE TYPE DESIGNED BY GEORGE AURIOL, CAST BY G. PEIGNOT ET FILS, PARIS

Le Grasset.

L'époque contemporaine semble, par ses recherches, vouloir trouver une nouvelle expression du vrai et du beau. Cependant, il est certaines personnes chez lesquelles le besoin d'un Art nouveau ne se fait pas sentir d'une façon bien intense. « Nos aînés, disent-ils, nous ont laissé de tels monuments d'art que nous ne pouvons espérer les surpasser. Pourquoi ne pas nous en tenir aux interprétations de ces chefs-d'œuvres. »

A cette objection, notre réponse semblera moins téméraire en nous aidant des déclarations qu'a faites le grand critique Taine, avec son autorité indubitable, dans sa *Philosophie de l'Art*. « L'œuvre d'art, dit-il, est déterminée par un ensemble qui est l'état général de l'esprit et des mœurs environnantes. » Plus loin il la définit ainsi : « Il y a une direction régnante qui est celle du siècle ; les talents qui voudraient pousser dans un autre sens trouvent l'issue fermée ; la pression de l'esprit public les comprime ou les dévie en leur imposant une floraison déterminée. » Et encore : « L'œuvre de l'artiste à laquelle auront contribué secrètement des millions de collaborateurs inconnus sera d'autant plus belle qu'outre son travail et son génie elle contiendra le génie et le travail du peuple qui l'entoure et des générations qui l'ont précédée. »

Laissons donc aux Elzévir, aux Fournier le Jeune et aux Didot la gloire d'avoir si merveilleusement résumé l'art typographique des xvie, xviiie et xixe siècles, et que notre œuvre à nous soit comme une résultante de la période contemporaine. Ce qui a toujours été le caractère dominant de l'art français, c'est ce souci de la clarté, de la précision, qui fait que dans ses diverses manifestations l'imagination n'a jamais empiété sur le domaine de la raison. Or, en observant le type dessiné par Eugène Grasset, ne retrouvons-nous pas l'indice de toutes ces qualités ? Tout d'abord, il est simple, c'est-à-dire qu'il n'y a rien qui soit superflu, rien qui ne vise pas uniquement à donner à chaque lettre ses caractères distinctifs. C'est pour ainsi dire la synthèse de la lettre indiquée au pinceau, sans déviations, sans inutilités, mais d'un trait sûr et ferme qui ne laisse rien au hasard.

TYPE AND ORNAMENTS DESIGNED BY GRASSET
CAST BY G. PEIGNOT ET FILS, PARIS

❡FASCICULUS I

 **OM SVAFLETS NATUR SÅSOM FOSSILT HARZ UTTRYCKT I FORMELN** CH⁴. O=CH³. HO=CH². H²O

TILL SVAFLETS ONTOGENI ELLER HÄRLEDNINGSHISTORIA

AN VID: håller att Svaflet är ett element och då jag frågar hvad man menar med ett ele: ment, sva: ras: — en kropp som ännu icke är sönderdelad. Man definierar sålunda med en negation och definitionen är sålun: da värdelös likasom begreppet element. ❡Jag påstod däremot med en viss be: stämdhet att Svaflet var ett sammansatt

ämne af analog konstitution med ett fos: silt Harz, ett Mineralharz, ett Brandharz, med ett ord: att Harz sålunda innehölle Kol, Väte, Syre eller var ett ÇHO utan att jag ville åtaga mig bestämma för: eningens proportioner. Och då man ut: fordrade mig att framlägga Kolet, Vätet och Syret svarade jag: vi tro ej på den absoluta identiteten utan nöja oss med analogier ledande till hög grad af sanno: likhet. I min egenskap af Aristoteles lär: junge tror jag icke så mycket på kroppar: nas konstitutiva olikheter utan mera på egenskapernas differenser under vissa gifna förutsättningar. I min egenskap af monist har jag tills vidare bundit mig vid antagandet att alla ämnen och alla krafter äro förvandta och om de äro här: ledda ur ett, de uppstått genom förtätning och förtunning, genom kopulation och korsning, genom arf och omvandling, genom urval och kamp, addition och sub: stitution och hvad mera man vill föreslå, men att jag därvid ej så strängt antagit den lagbundna ordningen, ändamålsen: ligheten och dylika sväfvande begrepp, hvilka jag dock fortfarande skulle vilja

PAGE FROM AUGUST STRINDBERG'S "ANTIBARBARUS," WITH DECO-
RATIONS BY ARTUR SJÖGREN. PRINTED BY BRÖDERNA LAGERSTRÖM

157

PAGE FROM AUGUST STRINDBERG'S "ANTIBARBARUS," WITH DECO-
RATIONS BY ARTUR SJÖGREN. PRINTED BY BRÖDERNA LAGERSTRÖM

hålla svätvande tills begreppen blifvit fullt utredda, eller hvad bättre är, af= lägsnade ur terminologien.

AG ÅTERVÄNDER nu till Svaflet och ställer upp min positiva analogi med ett harz emot den poetiska eller metafy= siska liknelsen med in= terimsbegreppet element, interims eme= dan man tillägger de viktiga orden »ännu icke» till ordet sönderdeladt.

℄Likasom ett Harz, CHO, är Svaflet vid vanlig temperatur:

Kristallinskt eller amorft;

Smältbart;

Olösligt i vatten;

Lösligt i Kolsvafla, Terpentin, kolväten etc.;

Brännbart;

Icke ledare af elektricitet;

Negativt elektriskt genom gnidning;

Smak- och luktlöst;

Sprödt;

Gifver syror (Bernstenssyra, Sylvius= syra);

Gifver med alkalier Harsåpor (=Svafvel= lefrar);

Gifver som syror salter med metalloxi= der, där Vätet substitueras af metallen.

℄Nu måste dessa likheter tagas med ett visst öfverseende, ty det finnes luktande harzer och icke luktande, kristalliniska och amorfa, och Svaflet själft är en sådan kameleont att det endast kan i ett visst gifvet moment gripas och ställas inför jämförelseprismat.

℄Men jag går vidare: vi veta att har= zerna tillhöra en naturlig familj som bör= jar med de ätheriska oljorna, sträcker sig öfver terpentiner och camphrar samt störtar å andra sidan ner till Kautschuck och Guttapercha. De ätheriska oljorna äro ju kolväten, hvilka uppgifvas lukta genom sin större vätehalt, då syrerika anses lukta mindre. Och de hafva alla, lik= som Terpentinoljan och Linoljan egen= skapen att förharzas genom uptagande af Syre.

℄Jag sätter digeln öfver elden och låter Svaflet smälta. Det flyter bernstens-gult *vid 115°* och nu först luktar det, men ej af Svafvel utan af Terpentin eller Harz när= mast dock Bonvax (=Vax och Terpentin). Temperaturen stiger, färgen går utåt spektrums röda ända, och blir orange, passerar hastigt det röda, så hastigt att orange lägger sig på det röda och ger blandfärgen rödbrunt vid 160°. En för= tätning, om kemisk eller fysisk, eller båda, har ägt rum och nu framträder en campherlukt. När jag första gången ob= serverade detta, trodde jag ej mitt kanske äldsta och kanske därför finast utveck= lade sinne, utan tillkallade min labora= torielärare, hvilken, jag säger det till hans heder, konstaterade faktum, och det utan att han ville förringa värdet af min iakttagelse genom att tala om för= oreningar. Och jag har sedan flerfaldiga gånger upprepat försöket i närvaro af trovärdiga vittnen.

℄Hvad har nu skett med Svaflet i digeln? En lång historia som här i förkortning kan uttryckas så, dock med starka reserva= tioner. Af värmen dissorierades Svaflet och blef ett ännu tämligen syrerikt Harz,

PAGE FROM AUGUST STRINDBERG'S "ANTIBARBARUS," WITH INITIAL LETTER BY ARTUR SJÖGREN. PRINTED BY BRÖDERNA LAGERSTRÖM

het ledes öfver glödande kol, man får Kolsyra; men om man leder svafvelångor öfver glödande kol, får man Kolsvafla. Öfver Kolsvaflans natur kämpades blodigt före midten af detta århundrade, och redan långt före trodde LAMPADIUS att Kolsvaflan bestod af Svafvel och Väte. Om han sagt Kol och Väte hade jag haft stöd för min mening att Kolsvaflan är ett kolväte analogt med Benzol.☞

☜ Hvarför jag tror att Kolsvaflan är en benzol? Därför att jag tror Svaflet bestå af Kol, Väte och Syre, finner jag det ytterst logiskt att när svafvelångor (icke Svafvelsyrlighet!) ledas öfver glödande kol, dessa ångor måste beröfvas sitt Syre och bli från CHO ett CH (harzernas sönderdelningsprodukter tillhöra ju mest benzolserien!). Och när Kolsvaflan besitter nästan alla en benzols egenskaper, finner jag mig berättigad godkänna antagandet. Absolut ren Kolsvafla är svafvelfri, luktar ätheriskt, behagligt (märk väl) som Benzol; har en mycket låg kokpunkt, är ytterst lätt antändlig, är olöslig i vatten, är starkt ljusbrytande, löser harzer, fetter, olja, Kautschuk, Svafvel etc. alldeles som Benzol. Ja dess fysiologiska verkningar äro äfven desamma, då dess ångor ger svindel, kongestioner, kräkningar etc. (se Eulenberg: Gewerbehygiene) alldeles som Benzol.

☜ Ur oren Kolsvafla fälles Svafvel i sol-

☞ Märk härtill att Benzolens, C_6H_6, atomsumma är 77,82 under det Kolsvaflans är 75,93. Hur skall jag krångla mig ur detta, utan att våldföra siffror? Jo, Benzolen har en kärna, som uppträder vid olika substitutionstillfällen, och denna heter C_6H_4 samt har Kolsvaflans atomsumma (molekularvikt) 75,82. Och när den uppträder i harzernas sönderdelningsprodukter Resorcin, Phtalsyra etc., så synes Kolsvaflan såsom en Svaflets sönderdelningsprodukt hjälpa mig betydligt vid bevisandet af Svaflets analogi med ett harz!

ljuset, det vet jag, men skulle äfven Svafvel fällas ur ren Kolsvafla, då är jag nödsakad tillgripa såsom nödfallsförklaring min försöksteori om *ancestrala energier*, hvilken jag velat spara till ett senare bref, men nu finner rådligast presentera och så formulera: Kroppar som en gång utgjort komposanter i en förening bibehålla föreningsenergien äfven såsom skilda.

☜ Exempel: — Antag att Svafvel är Kol, Väte, Syre i vissa förhållanden. Låt det glödande kolet dissociera dessa och borttaga Syret, så bibehålla i det nu supponerade återstående kolvätet Kolet och Väte sin ärfda benägenhet att med ett nytt Syre, ur luften hämtadt till exempel, åter bilda Svafvel och ej något annat COH, såsom Cellulosa, Socker, Stärkelse, Linolja, Alkohol eller dyl.

☜ Corollarium: Därför är Svaflets ifriga uppträdande i djur och växtkroppar beroende af en Svaflets bildning af Kol, Väte och Syre, antingen dessa förr gjort sin metempsykos i svafvelsyrade salter, vätesvafla eller svafvelalkalier etcetera.

☜ Jag har nu kommit så långt att jag i fjärran ser Kolsvaflan som ett kolväte, men måste bekänna att jag haft ögonblick, då jag trott den vara en alkohol, icke därför att den i farmakopéerna länge kallades Svafvelalkohol, utan af andra grunder. Hvad som passerar i det glö-

PAGE FROM AUGUST STRINDBERG'S "ANTIBAR-
BARUS." PRINTED BY BRÖDERNA LAGERSTRÖM

Die Märchen
der
Weltliteratur

Herausgegeben von
Prof. Dr. Friedrich von der Leyen=
München und Dr. Paul Zaunert=
Marburg

Die Ausstattung besorgte
F. H. Ehmcke

Carl Michael
Bellman ?
Fredmans ?
? Episteln ?
Aus dem Schwedi=
schen übertragen
von Felix Niedner
Mit Einführung
von Gustav Kaethe
1 bis 12tes Tausend
Jena 1909/verlegt bei
Eugen Diederichs

TITLE-PAGES DESIGNED BY PROF. F. H. EHMCKE
PUBLISHED BY EUGEN DIEDERICHS

TITLE-PAGES DESIGNED BY PROF. F. H. EHMCKE
PUBLISHED BY EUGEN DIEDERICHS

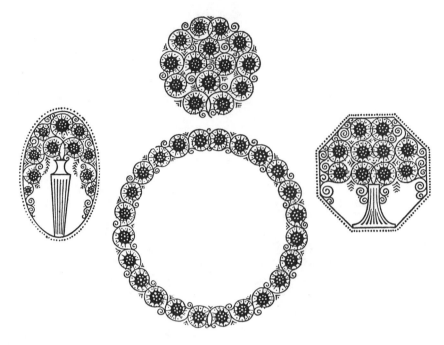

ORNAMENTS DESIGNED BY PROF. F. W. KLEUKENS, FOR THE BAUERSCHE GIESSEREI, FRANKFURT A.M.

ORNAMENTS DESIGNED BY PROF. WALTER TIEMANN, FOR GEBR. KLINGSPOR, OFFENBACH A.M.

INITIAL LETTERS AND ORNAMENTS DESIGNED BY PROF. F. W. KLEUKENS, FOR D. STEMPEL, FRANKFURT A.M.

HEAD-PIECES BY EMIL PREETORIUS FOR DAUDET'S "TARTARIN DE
TARASCON." PUBLISHED BY DER GELBE VERLAG, MÜNCHEN-DACHAU

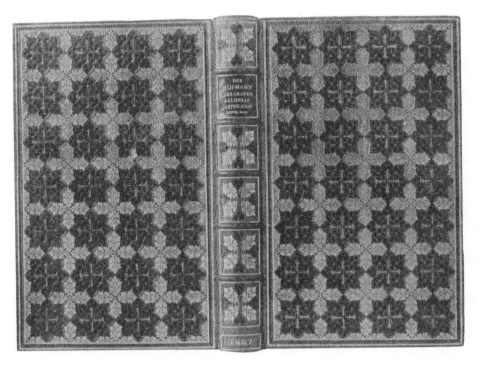

BOOKBINDING IN GREEN MOROCCO, WITH GOLD AND BLACK TOOLING
DESIGNED BY P. A. DEMETER, EXECUTED BY HÜBEL AND DENCK

BOOKBINDING IN LEMON YELLOW MOROCCO, WITH GREEN INLAY AND GOLD TOOLING
DESIGNED BY P. A. DEMETER, EXECUTED BY HÜBEL AND DENCK

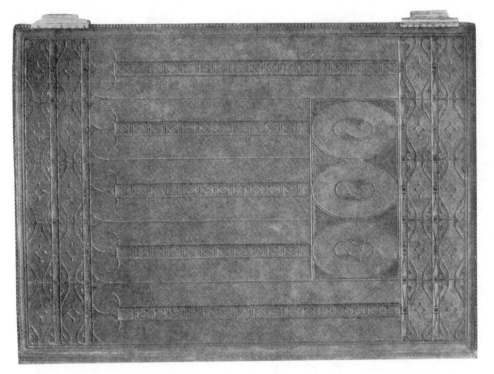

BOOKBINDING IN BROWN LEATHER, WITH BLIND TOOLING. DESIGNED BY
PROF. JOH. VINCENZ CISSARZ, EXECUTED BY AD. BÜHLER

BOOKBINDING IN GREEN MOROCCO, WITH GOLD TOOLING. DESIGNED BY P. A. DEMETER
EXECUTED BY HUBEL AND DENCK

169

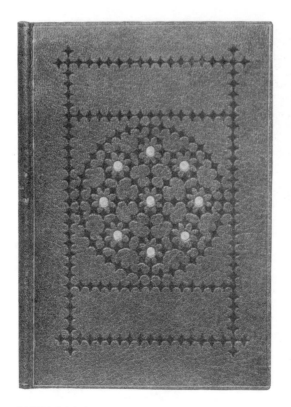

BOOKBINDING IN ORANGE YELLOW MOROCCO, WITH INLAY
AND BLIND TOOLING. BY PAUL KERSTEN

BOOKBINDING IN NEAT'S LEATHER, WITH PUNCHED
AND TANNED ORNAMENTATION. BY PAUL KERSTEN

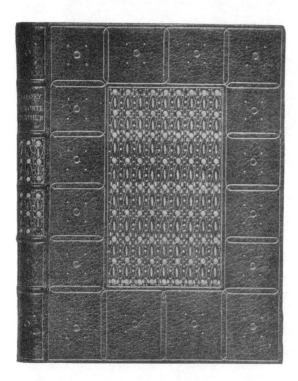

BOOKBINDING IN RED MOROCCO, WITH INLAY AND GOLD
TOOLING. BY PAUL KERSTEN

BOOKBINDING IN BLUE MOROCCO, WITH INLAY AND
GOLD TOOLING. BV PAUL KERSTEN

170

BOOKBINDING IN BUFF MOROCCO, WITH INLAY
AND GOLD TOOLING. BY PAUL KERSTEN

BOOKBINDING IN BLUE MOROCCO, WITH INLAY
AND GOLD TOOLING. BY PAUL KERSTEN

BOOKBINDING IN RED CALF, WITH INLAY AND GOLD
TOOLING. BY PAUL KERSTEN

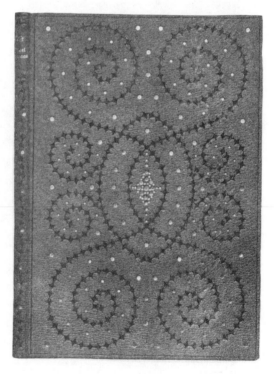

BOOKBINDING IN PIGSKIN, WITH TOOLING.
BY PAUL KERSTEN

BOOKBINDING IN VELLUM, WITH GILT ORNAMENTATION. DESIGNED BY
PROF. HUGO STEINER-PRAG, EXECUTED BY HÜBEL AND DENCK

BOOKBINDING IN DARK BLUE CALF, WITH GOLD TOOLING. DESIGNED BY
PROF. HUGO STEINER-PRAG, EXECUTED BY HÜBEL AND DENCK

172

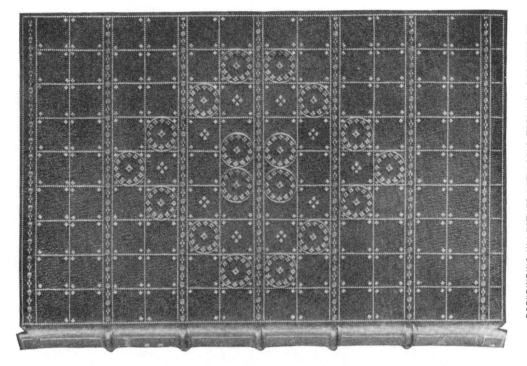

173

BOOKBINDING IN LEATHER, WITH SILVER CLASPS. DESIGNED BY PROF.
JOH. VINCENZ CISSARZ, EXECUTED BY KARL STRENGER

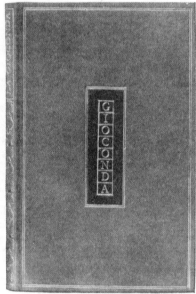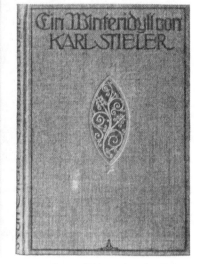

BOOKBINDINGS IN LEATHER, WITH GOLD TOOLING. DESIGNED BY PROF. JOH.
VINCENZ CISSARZ, EXECUTED BY GUSTAV FRÖLICH

BINDING-CASE. DESIGNED BY
PROF. JOH. VINCENZ CISSARZ

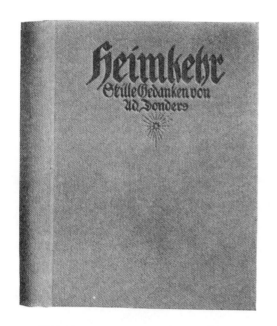

BINDING-CASE. DESIGNED BY KARL KÖSTER

VELLUM BINDING. DESIGNED BY KARL KÖSTER

VELLUM BINDING, WITH BATIK ORNAMENTATION
DESIGNED BY KARL KÖSTER

BOOKBINDING IN LEATHER, WITH GOLD TOOLING
DESIGNED BY KARL KÖSTER

EOOKBINDING IN WHITE PIGSKIN, WITH INLAY AND GOLD TOOLING
BY FRANZ WEISSE

BOOKBINDING IN NATURAL COLOURED PIGSKIN, WITH
BLIND TOOLING. BV FRANZ WEISSE

PARCHMENT BINDING, WITH BATIK ORNAMENTATION
BY FRANZ WEISSE

HALF-CALF AND PAPER BINDING. DESIGNED BY RUDOLF KOCH

VELLUM BINDING. DESIGNED BY RUDOLF KOCH

179

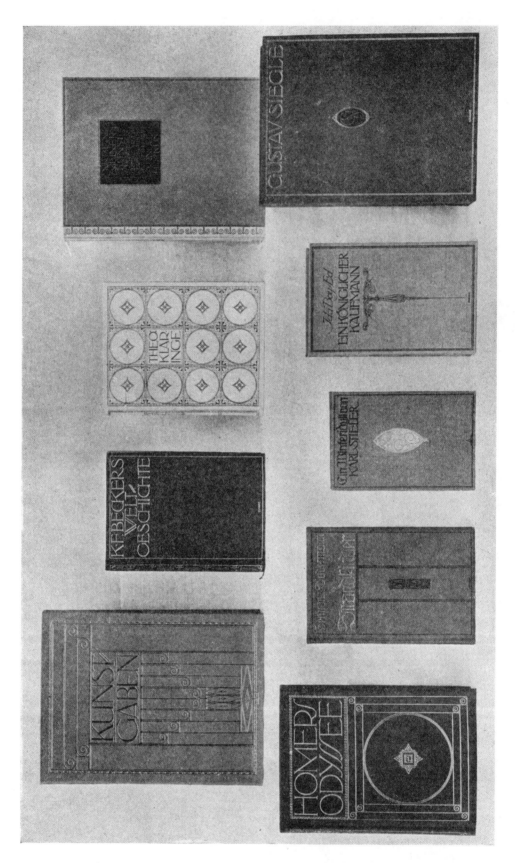

BINDING-CASES IN LEATHER AND CLOTH. DESIGNED BY PROF. JOH. VINCENZ CISSARZ

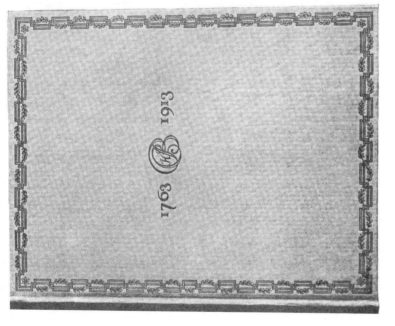

BINDING-CASE.   DESIGNED BY PAUL RENNER

DESIGNED BY PROF. EMANUEL VON SEIDL

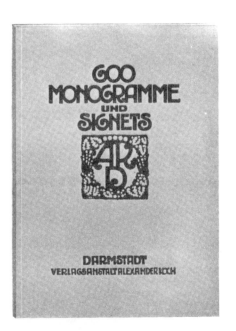

DESIGNED BY "L"

DESIGNED BY FRITZ SCHOLL

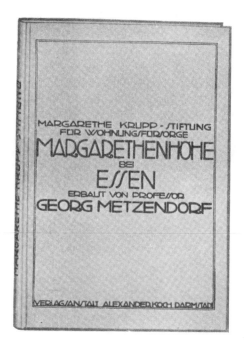

DESIGNED BY EMANUEL JOSEPH MARGOLD

BINDING-CASES DESIGNED FOR
ALEXANDER KOCH, DARMSTADT

PAPER COVERS.   DESIGNED BY EMIL PREETORIUS

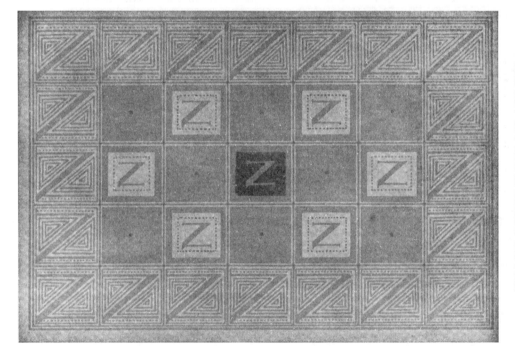

186

FRANCE

THE ART OF THE BOOK IN FRANCE. BY E. A. TAYLOR

LINGERING in thought over the far-away days of the glorious bibliographic and typographical past that France has enjoyed, one finds little has happened, amidst all the changes which have swept over those arts in recent years, to disturb the employment of her bibliopegic artists. There are few of her remaining old streets through which one passes without being attracted in one way or another to the sign of the *relieur-doreur*. To give a remarkable instance of this unique position one has only to recall the sale of the collection of the Vicomte de la Croix-Laval in 1902, in which the books were not catalogued in the names of the author but in that of the bookbinder. But this is not surprising when we consider the excellent craftsmanship of such men as G. Canape, Chambolle-Duru, S. David, Charles Lanoë, Marius Michel, G. Mercier, René Kieffer, and the fascinating execution of the designs on vellum by André Mare. Yet it is not uncommon to hear the travellers' comment that books with an attractive outside appearance are non-existent in Paris. Unlike England, France expends little additional labour on the lasting, apart from the certain attractive qualities of cloth or paper-covered board casings, while modern end-papers, as known in other countries, have so far found little consideration. Much energy is focussed on the *edition de luxe*, embodying the work of popular artists, good paper and type, the result being a limited number of paper-covered volumes, all excellently produced, but very often disappointing in their page arrangement and design and the suitability of text to type and type to illustration. But this leads me into an explanatory discussion on the old printer's independence of other craftsmen whose art is now divided into separate and recognised trades. And it is remarkable that it should be so to such a great extent, for fewer places other than Paris are so sympathetically enjoined to their artists. It may be the fault of the artist who is more enwrapped in his craft than the art evolved in its ultimate end. Within the last few years, however, printing has vastly improved, and this has been due in no small measure to the efforts of MM. G. Peignot and Sons. As early as 1900 the Peignot type foundry introduced a new typography with frankly modern tendencies, the best testimony of their efforts at that time being the productions of "Grasset," following with the "Auriol," and later on the Bellery-Desfontaines types and ornaments. At the same time, not desiring to lose touch with that which in typography of the past is most intrinsically valuable for to-day, a little booklet issued lately, entitled "Les Cochins," by the two brothers Peignot, clearly demonstrates the results of their attainment. This booklet, apart from being a catalogue of their research, has behind it the primary desire that editors and printers should try to realise the significance of a typographical revival in France, and the influence it would have on all branches of the graphic arts. ✠ Despite the remarkable progress that process work has made, apart from the most ingenious inventions and machinery being of French origin, wood-engravers and wood-engraving, as employed for illustrative purposes, maintain a prominent and more unique position in France than in any other European country. Amongst the most recent productions of note " Daphnis et Chloé" (p. 199), printed and published by M. L. Pichon, is uncommonly good, in fact all that issues from M. Pichon's little establishment is unusually refined. Then there are others, but space will not permit me to dwell on each one's excellent qualities. However, I must not neglect to mention the remarkable edition of " Le Grand Testament de François Villon," which I have seen in preparation by M. A. M. Peignot, with illustrations and especially designed type by Bernard Naudin ; also some thoughtful little volumes in the series " Les Maîtres du Livre," published by MM. Georges Crès et Cie under the direction of M. Ad. van Bever ; and if it were not for the thoughtful, untiring efforts of such editors as M. Lucien Vogel, of the " Gazette du Bon Ton," and publishers of *éditions d'art* as MM. A. Blaizot, L. Carteret, H. Floury, F. Ferroud, Jules Meynial, R. Helleu, René Kieffer, E. Rey, Octave Charpentier, E. Lévy, and H. Piazza, the bibliophiles of Paris would have a poor output from which to select. From amongst others the notable and varied publications of the libraries Ollendorff, Larousse, Hachette et Cie, A. Fayard et Cie, Calman Levy, Plon-Nourrit et Cie, Adrian Sporck, L. Michaud, E. Flammarion and A. Vaillant should be noted. Finally I must not forget to mention the powerful influence of the " Société des Amis des Livres," " Les Cent Bibliophiles," the " Société Normande du Livre illustré," and the "Société du Livre d'Art Contemporain" ; and without a prolonged description of each *Société* it must suffice to mention the prosperity the " Société des Amis des Livres " enjoys under the presidency of M. Henri Beraldi, the originator of the " Société des Bibliophiles de Paris" and a publisher of note. Amongst his first efforts " Paysages Parisiens," by Emile Goudeau, and G. Montorgueil's " Paris au Hasard," both illustrated by Auguste Lepère, are the most distinguished, and to him my thanks are due for his kindly interest in my bibliographical quest, and to the President of " Les Cent Bibliophiles," M. Eugène Rodrigues, for his generosity in placing at my disposal pages and illustrations from his admirable collection. ✠ After all, it is to men like these, and to the organizations to which they belong, that France owes the prominent bibliographical position she holds, and the freedom her excellent artists and craftsmen enjoy in retaining for us in fitting garb the minds of the great, be they echoes of the past or turbulent cries in the dark, the songs of the open and sunlight, the sonnets of autumn and shade, or the love in the laughter of children.

LE DERNIER LIVRE D'ÉDOUARD PELLETAN.

Voici donc le point final mis à la page et voici le dernier feuillet
tourné! Nul livre désormais ne portera cette firme réputée, ornée de
la devise empruntée à Thucydide : ΚΤΗΜΑ ΕΣ ΑΕΙ. De même qu'il
n'y a plus d'éditeur, il n'y aura plus d'éditions Pelletan.

Avec quel amour, avec quels soins, pourtant, le maître a travaillé
à ce dernier fils de son génie! Cet ouvrage, tout en gravures origi-
nales, était avec *La Rôtisserie,* toute en gravures de reproduction, les
deux livres qu'il affectionnait le plus. Dans *La Rôtisserie de la Reine
Pédauque,* il avait écrit, en quelque sorte, le testament de la gravure
sur bois d'interprétation, et, par l'illustration et l'habillage du texte,
posé le sceau sur les ouvrages de cet ordre. *La Rôtisserie* reste le livre
du xixᵉ siècle, *Hésiode* et *La Terre & l'Homme* appartiennent au xxᵉ.
Plus d'illustrations proprement dites, mais une suite de libres compositions, parentes du texte par leur sentiment général, — et une page
renouvelée, qu'égaient des bandeaux de couleurs, qu'une extraordi-
naire abondance de sujets décore. Le grec de Garamond qui, depuis
plus de quarante ans, dormait dans les casses de l'Imprimerie natio-
nale, apporte la séduction de son écriture fleurie; en regard, les pages
de la traduction, en caractères romains de même origine, se disposent
avec noblesse. Et, quand on arrive à la partie moderne, l'aspect
change. Le texte de M. Anatole France s'y déroule comme un fleuve
entre les cent îlots des gravures. Puis, çà et là, aux endroits choisis,
de grandes compositions en pleine page. Partout, un ordre évident et
une richesse non moins évidente. Chaque livre de Pelletan est pareil
à la salle d'un musée bien disposé; la salle d'*Hésiode* et de *La Terre &
l'Homme* est une des plus somptueuses et des plus étranges. Son grec,

PAGE PRINTED IN "GARAMOND" TYPE (ENGRAVED
FOR FRANÇOIS I), WITH WOODCUT BY PAUL EMILE
COLIN, LENT BY MONS. R. HELLEU

LE TRANSFORMISME

DES origines de la terre à l'apparition de l'homme, le développement des formes est pareil à celui de l'arbre. Les organismes définis sont les feuilles éparpillées, les fruits naissants et les fruits mûrs, les fruits tombés, les fleurs ouvertes. Plus bas les rameaux indistincts, les branches frustes, le tronc massif, les racines perdues qui lient la forme épanouie à la substance originelle. Ainsi, les formes de la vie qui cherchent l'équilibre à la clarté de la conscience, tendent à se différencier de la forme de l'univers. La terre est nue à l'origine, et paraît nue encore à l'heure où la vie essentielle s'élabore au fond de la mer. Puis, les forces intérieures se révèlent à sa surface en végétaux gras et confus, en bêtes chaotiques où le sol attache le poids des alluvions primitives ; puis ce sont de hautes forêts qui répandent dans le ciel libre leurs bras chargés de feuilles vertes, ce sont d'harmonieux animaux ; l'homme apparaît, s'efforçant d'ordonner son être, de marier son rythme intérieur au rythme entier de la nature ; enfin l'esprit veut s'affranchir, dominer les lois de la vie : les lois de la vie le suppriment. Or, l'intelligence des hommes prend contact avec la nature en suivant les mêmes chemins. De son éveil à son éclosion, à ses éclipses périodiques, elle répète mot à mot l'histoire des âges confus qui l'ont précédé sur la terre. L'artiste primitif laisse engagées dans la forme du monde les architectures transitoires, hommes, bêtes et plantes, où la substance de la vie fleurit pour un moment. Dans leurs manifestations brutes, tous les archaïsmes se touchent, l'esprit humain n'a qu'un berceau. La forme des statues antiques est emprisonnée dans la pierre, comme ces monstres indistincts que le sol ne veut pas quitter et dont il empâte toujours les articulations épaisses. En elles, pesamment, circule une vie torpide et muette, une chaleur qui n'est pas flamme encore : dans sa matrice de granit, le germe de l'esprit tressaille.

PAGE PRINTED IN ROMAN FACE TYPE DESIGNED BY GEORGE AURIOL, CAST BY G. PEIGNOT ET FILS, PARIS

E ne saurais approuver cette lâche espèce d'hommes qui mesurent la durée de leur affection à celle de la félicité de leurs amis; et pour moi, bien loin d'être d'une humeur si basse, je me pique d'aimer jusques en la prison et dans le sépulcre. J'en ai rendu des témoignages publics durant la plus chaude persécution de ce grand et divin Théophile, et j'ai fait voir que, parmi l'infidélité du siècle où nous sommes, il se trouve encore des amitiés assez généreuses pour mépriser tout ce que les autres craignent; mais, puisque sa mort m'a ravi le moyen de le servir, je veux donner à sa mémoire les soins que j'avais destinés à sa personne, et faire voir à la postérité que, pourvu que l'ignorance des imprimeurs ne mette point de faute à des ouvrages qui d'eux-mêmes n'en ont pas une, elle ne saurait rien avoir qui puisse égaler ce qu'ils valent. ...Quiconque achètera ce digne livre, sans doute sera contraint d'avouer que c'est la première fois qu'il a bien lu Théophile. De sorte que je ne fais pas difficulté de publier hautement que tous les morts ni tous les vivants n'ont rien qui puisse approcher des forces de ce vigoureux génie; et si, parmi les derniers, il se rencontre quelque extravagant qui juge que j'offense sa gloire imaginaire, pour lui montrer que je le crains autant comme je l'estime, je veux qu'il sache que je m'appelle   DE SCUDÉRY.

147

PAGE PRINTED IN "NICOLAS COCHIN" TYPE, ADAPTED
AND CAST BY G. PEIGNOT ET FILS, PARIS

C'était, il m'en souvient, par une nuit d'automne,
Triste et froide, à peu près semblable à celle-ci ;
Le murmure du vent, de son bruit monotone,
Dans mon cerveau lassé berçait mon noir souci.
J'étais à la fenêtre, attendant ma maîtresse ;
Et, tout en écoutant dans cette obscurité,
Je me sentais dans l'âme une telle détresse,
Qu'il me vint le soupçon d'une infidélité.
La rue où je logeais était sombre et déserte ;
Quelques ombres passaient, un falot à la main ;
Quand la bise soufflait dans la porte entr'ouverte,
On entendait de loin comme un soupir humain.
Je ne sais, à vrai dire, à quel fâcheux présage
Mon esprit inquiet alors s'abandonna.
Je rappelais en vain un reste de courage,
Et me sentis frémir lorsque l'heure sonna.
Elle ne venait pas. Seul, la tête baissée,
Je regardai longtemps les murs et le chemin, —
Et je ne t'ai pas dit quelle ardeur insensée
Cette inconstante femme allumait en mon sein ;
Je n'aimais qu'elle au monde, et vivre un jour sans elle
Me semblait un destin plus affreux que la mort.
Je me souviens pourtant qu'en cette nuit cruelle
Pour briser mon lien je fis un long effort.
Je la nommai cent fois perfide et déloyale,
Je comptai tous les maux qu'elle m'avait causés.
Hélas ! au souvenir de sa beauté fatale,
Quels maux et quels chagrins n'étaient pas apaisés !
Le jour parut enfin. — Las d'une vaine attente,

PAGE FROM A. DE MUSSET'S "LES NUITS" (JULES MEYNIAL,
PARIS), PRINTED IN TYPE DESIGNED BY ADOLPHE GIRALDON
CAST BY LA MAISON DEBERNY

Deux causes essentielles ont produit cet effet. D'abord, et bien visiblement, une morbidesse native le prédestinait aux émotions aiguës, voluptés ou tourments : la frénésie d'aimer trépide en ses premiers poèmes, tout comme la fureur de se tourmenter exaspérera les derniers. Donc, à corps perdu, l'adolescent s'est rué à la joie : il y tord et use ses nerfs, si bien qu'il en arrive avant l'heure à l'épuisement des énergies vitales, qui sera la seconde cause de son abattement. A cette étape de sa vie, pour que la crise se manifeste, il suffira de quelque amour trompé, événement banal, prévu, et dont il devisait naguère sans amertume, mais qui, cette fois, coïncide avec un état de réceptivité anormale; la volonté ne réagit plus, et le blessé, beaucoup moins blessé que malade, accepte son sort, adopte sa destinée, concentre en elle ses facultés pensantes comme ses facultés nerveuses, et délibérément se couche sur son lit d'incurable, pour crier jusqu'à ce qu'il en meure.

A parler franc, et pour tout dire, Musset avait reconnu dans sa douleur la source même de son génie; ce besoin de souffrance, qui déjà lui était devenu naturel, allait ainsi lui devenir précieux. Est-ce un jugement téméraire, de considérer que cet amoureux au désespoir ait eu la prétention de s'ériger en personnage de légende et d'incarner, dans la mémoire des hommes, le type de l'amant au dix-neuvième siècle? Les grandes passions, en somme, sont assez rares; l'amour total, exclusif, absolu, ne se rencontre guère que dans les livres ; chaque siècle à peine nous en donne un: Héloïse et Abeilard, Dante et Béatrice, Laure et Pétrarque, Roméo et Juliette, puis, toute seule, Manon Lescaut ou Mlle de Lespinasse, et Musset tout seul... Pourquoi pas? Il s'égale, en pensée, aux illustres romans d'amour; à lui seul il sera le poème et le poète tout à la fois, l'œuvre vécue, une monographie du désespoir chanté, l'inoubliable, l'unique, et sans que même un nom de femme s'accroche à l'auréole du sien... Oui, pourquoi pas ? Et poétiquement, avec une complaisance d'exception, il s'aide à la douleur. Guérir? Il ne le voudrait pas! Au besoin, des poisons l'empêcheront

PAGE FROM A. DE MUSSET'S "LES NUITS" (JULES MEYNIAL, PARIS). PRINTED IN TYPE DESIGNED BY ADOLPHE GIRALDON CAST BY LA MAISON DEBERNY

du trespas de leur maistre. Apres que Dorcon
fut enterré Chloé mena Daphnis en la caverne des
Nymphes, où elle le nettoya, et quant et quant pour
la premiere fois en presence de Daphnis lava aussi
son beau corps d'elle-mesme, blanc et poly comme
albastre, et qui n'avoit que faire d'estre lavé pour
sembler beau, puis en cueillant ensemble des fleurs
que portoit la saison, en firent des chappeaux aux
images des Nymphes, et attacherent contre la
roche la fluste de Dorcon pour offrande, puis cela
faict retournerent vers leurs chevres et brebis, lesquelles ils trouverent toutes tapies contre la terre
sans paistre ny besler, pour l'ennuy et le regret
qu'elles avoyent, ainsi qu'il est à presumer, de ne
veoir plus ny Daphnis ny Chloé, mais aussi-tost
qu'elles les apperçeurent, et qu'eux se prindrent à
les sifler comme de coustume, et à joüer du fla-
geollet, elles se leverent incontinent, et se prindrent
à pasturer comme devant, et les chevres à sauteler

PAGE FROM "DAPHNIS ET CHLOÉ." PRINTED IN "JENSON"
TYPE BY L. PICHON, PARIS, WITH WOODCUT BY CARLÈGLE

BOOKBINDING IN LEVANT MOROCCO, WITH INLAY AND TOOLING
DESIGNED BY ADOLPHE GIRALDON, EXECUTED BY G. CANAPE

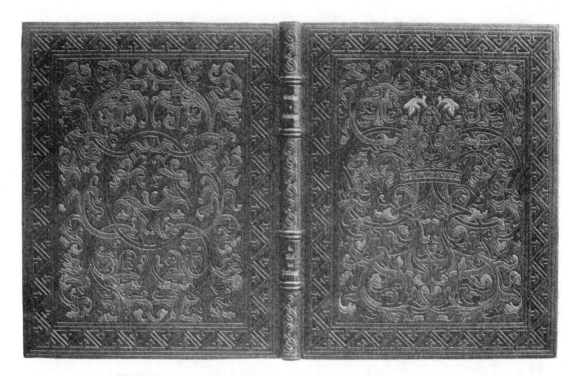

BOOKBINDING IN LEVANT MOROCCO, WITH INLAY AND TOOLING. BY G. CANAPE

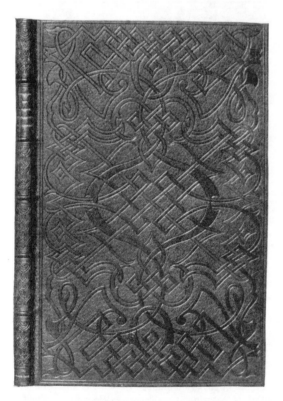 

BOOKBINDINGS IN LEVANT MOROCCO, WITH INLAY AND TOOLING. BY CHAMBOLLE-DURU

BOOKBINDING IN RED MOROCCO, WITH INLAY AND GOLD TOOLING.   BY S. DAVID

BOOKBINDING IN MOROCCO, WITH GOLD TOOLING.   BY S. DAVID

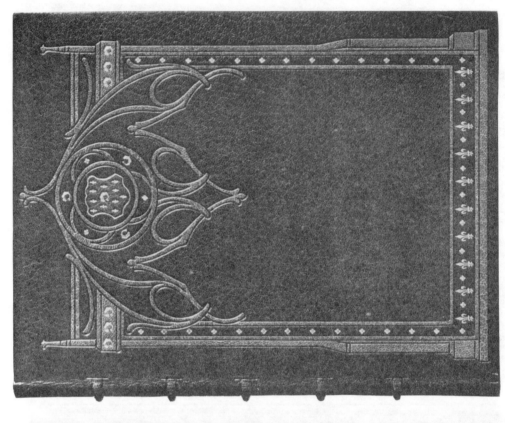

BOOKBINDING IN DARK BLUE FRENCH MOROCCO, WITH INLAY AND GOLD TOOLING.
BY S. DAVID

BOOKBINDING IN GREEN MOROCCO, WITH INLAY AND GOLD TOOLING
BY RENÉ KIEFFER

BOOKBINDING IN FRENCH MOROCCO, WITH GOLD TOOLING
DESIGNED BY J. DE LA NÉZIÈRE, EXECUTED BY DURVAND
(In the possession of Mons. H. Piazza)

BOOKBINDING IN FRENCH MOROCCO, WITH INLAY AND GOLD TOOLING
DESIGNED BY ETIENNE DINET, EXECUTED BY DURVAND
(In the possession of Mons. H. Piazza)

205

BOOKBINDING IN PARCHMENT, TOOLED AND COLOURED
BY ANDRÉ MARE
(In the possession of Mons. Paul Aaam)

BOOKBINDING IN PARCHMENT, TOOLED AND COLOURED. BY ANDRÉ MARE
(In the possession of Mons. L. Vauxcelles)

BOOKBINDING IN PARCHMENT, TOOLED
AND COLOURED. BY ANDRÉ MARE

BOOKBINDING IN BLUE MOROCCO, WITH INLAY AND GOLD TOOLING
DESIGNED BY A. SEGAUD, EXECUTED BY P. SOUZE
(Lent by Maison Hachette & Cie)

BINDING-CASE DESIGNED BY G. AURIOL. FOR MAISON LAROUSSE

BINDING-CASE DESIGNED BY LUCIEN LAFORGE
FOR MAISON LAROUSSE

BINDING-CASE DESIGNED BY G. AURIOL
FOR MAISON LAROUSSE

209

AUSTRIA

THE ART OF THE BOOK IN AUSTRIA
BY A. S. LEVETUS

L IKE other countries Austria has, in all that relates to the book, gone through periods of high developments, followed by a time of inactivity which could but lead to eventual decay. That in the past many works of a high artistic value as regards printing, illustrations, type, and binding, in fact all the qualities which go to make an artistic production, were issued by the various presses, many books still existing go to prove. On the whole the printers of Austria were never very numerous, and she has never been a book-producing centre, even in the Capital itself, as have been many German cities, such as Nuremberg, Augsburg and Leipzig. Under the Empress Maria Theresa the art of the book flourished, for being possessed of a fine artistic nature, she granted many privileges to the makers of books, and set great value on such volumes as were real works of art. Her son, Joseph II, who during his youth, following the custom of the time, adopted a trade, chose printing, and mastered it thoroughly. He likewise granted certain privileges to the printers and in every way encouraged the art. During the second half of the eighteenth century the Art of the Book developed considerably. New types were invented, woodcut engravings gave way to copper engravings, the paper was of the best quality, the bindings of the finest leather and of beautiful design, everything, including the endpapers, reached the highest standard. But reaction was inevitable in Austria as it was in other countries, for the age of machinery had come. Hand-made paper, which had furnished a staple trade in Moravia since 1520, when the first paper-mill was founded in Gross-Ullersdorf, deteriorated ; the printing-machine took the

TITLE-PAGE DESIGNED BY R. RŮŽIČKA. PUBLISHED BY THE
MANES SOCIETY, PRAGUE

213

place of the hand-press ; the fine hand-tooled leather bindings were forced to yield to the more commercial article. ✠ But in Austria, as elsewhere, the Art of the Book was to be reborn, and it was William Morris who was to give the impulse, for the fame of the Kelmscott Press had reached Vienna. The men of the new school, Alfred Roller, Josef Hoffmann, Koloman Moser, Baron Myrbach, Rudolf von Larisch, and others have spread the new teaching. The moment was the right one, the need of reform in all and everything concerning book-production was recognised as part of the programme when the general question of the teaching of art was raised in 1897 ; but the regeneration of the Art of the Book really dated from the beginning of the present century. It must not be thought that no efforts had been made to rescue the art previous to the great reform. Far from it. Twenty-five years ago the first steps were taken by the founding of the Imperial "Lehr -und Versuchsanstalt für graphische Kunst," an institution for teaching and experimenting in graphic art, where from the first excellent work was done under Hofrat Eder. The "Hof -und Staats-druckerei" (Imperial and State Printing Office) had been called into existence eighty years previously. But the great impetus was given some dozen years ago when men trained in the new school of thought in decorative art were appointed teachers in the various schools and institutions. ✠ The Art of the Book in Austria in its modern aspect is but young, but its development is most interesting. All that is best in graphic art of the past served as the ground-work on which to build the art of our time ; and this artistic basis being of so fine a calibre, sound and sure, has led to very satisfactory results. First, in the teaching of ornamental writing under Professor Rudolf von Larisch. He has expounded his tenets in his "Unterricht in ornamentaler Schrift," a work of great

TITLE-PAGE DESIGNED BY VLADIMÍR ŽUPANSKÝ. PUBLISHED BY THE MANES SOCIETY, PRAGUE

value to all interested in this subject. What he aims at is form, configuration and spacing, to add rhythm to the letters themselves, and to harmonise one with another in the building-up of the word ; for even the simplest of words rightly rendered should be decorative. He does not consider the creating of new forms of paramount importance, but sets much store on the relation of the letter to the word, the word to the sentence. These should fit into one another in the same manner as the component parts of a perfect piece of architecture, for, as in architecture we see the foundation of all art, so in lettering the basis of all book decoration is to be sought. This theory is supported by the study of early printed works and more particularly so in those printed towards the end of the sixteenth century. Here we see the aim was to achieve harmony in type, ornament and illustration. This, too, is the aim of those who produce artistic books other than those issued by the ordinary publisher. Unfortunately there are but few of the former class in Austria. But many of the Austrian artists are engaged in illustrating books for German and other publishers. In Vienna, Artur Wolf has published some very fine works illustrated by Franz von Bayros, Ferdinand Staeger, and other artists; Konegen's series of children's books, illustrated by Marianne Hitschmann-Steinberger, are full of charm and understanding of child life ; Gerlach and Wiedling's books for children have been illustrated by various artists: Professor Czeschka, Karl Fahringer, F. Staeger, Franz Wacik, Fräulein Frimberger among others. That excellent work is being done may be gathered from our illustrations. Fräulein C. Hasselwander has done very good work as an illustrator of children's stories ; C. Köystrand has won renown as an illustrator of refined humour; Ferdinand Staeger is one of the best-known illustrators of the " Münchner Jugend," and a draughtsman of great

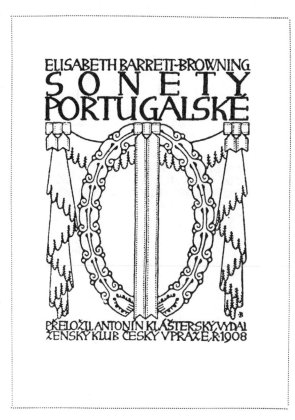

TITLE-PAGE DESIGNED BY J. BENDA. PUBLISHED BY THE ŽENSKÝ KLUB, PRAGUE

215

variety and vitality; Wenzel Oswald and Gustav Kalhammer are past students of the Imperial "Kunstgewerbeschule" in Vienna and are essentially decorative in their art; while Dagobert Peche hails from the Imperial Academy and his work is of a highly decorative character. Alfred Keller is an architect by profession, as is Dagobert Peche, but he is also an illustrator of books, his chief *forte* lying in line drawing. ✠ Some of the Austrian artists excel in the designing of book-bindings, and it is safe to say their

PAGE DESIGNED BY HEDWIG SCHMIEDL, FOR THE IMPERIAL GRAPHISCHE LEHR-UND VERSUCHSANSTALT, VIENNA

work will achieve lasting fame. The mention of names such as Professors Josef Hoffmann, Koloman Moser and Czeschka, are sufficient to vouch for this assertion; Anton Hofer and Rudolf Geyer, both past students of the Imperial Arts and Crafts School, have also done some very beautiful work which will live. All these artists have produced bindings which in quality of design, material, and workmanship are all that could be desired. ✠ In the designing of new types excellent results have been achieved. "Czeschka's Antiqua," the invention of Professor Czeschka, is extremely beautiful in its simplicity. It has been acquired by Messrs. Genzsch and Heyse, of Hamburg, and is illustrated on page 211. ✠ Dr. Rudolf Junk's new type is characterized by the same high qualities though it differs widely in form from that of Professor Czeschka;

PAGE DESIGNED BY BERTA BINDTNER, FOR THE IMPERIAL GRAPHISCHE LEHR-UND VERSUCHSANSTALT, VIENNA

COVER DESIGN BY F. KYSELA, FOR NOVA EDICE, PRAGUE

Herr Mader's type is less clear, though it is interesting. For this Professor Hoffmann has made the borders and ornament. Fräulein Schmidt may also be counted amongst those who have created new and interesting types. These have all been published by the " Hof -und Staatsdruckerei." In the provinces Bohemia holds the first place in the Art of the Book, which is but natural considering how high a prestige Prague, Pilsen, Kuttenberg, and other of her towns enjoyed in bygone ages. In modern graphic art and book-decoration many Czech artists have distinguished themselves. The various reproductions here show that their inspirations are those of the true artist. To these must be added Zdenka Braunerová, Adolf Kašpar, and Vojtěch Preissig. That the publishers are collaborating with the artists is a good sign, and the next few years will no doubt see further developments. The fact that the modern movement in Bohemia in the Art of the Book is still in its infancy, and that, in spite of this, so much that is good has already been done, speaks well for the future.

TAILPIECE DESIGNED BY HEDWIG SCHMIEDL, FOR THE IMPERIAL GRAPHISCHE LEHR -UND VERSUCHSANSTALT, VIENNA

ORNAMENT BY WENZEL OSWALD

KNIHA JE VĚNOVÁNA MNOHOVÁŽENÉ NADĚŽDĚ NIKOLAJEVNĚ KRAMÁŘOVÉ

Milostivá paní, vzpomínám na ony hodiny, kdy poprvé jste naslouchala torsům této knihy, tam daleko na jižním břehu Svojí vlasti, vynořujícím se jako pohádka z bílých pěn Siného moře, žijí v jasné vzpomínce ony šťastné, slunné dny, pod jejichž nebem zrálo mé dílo, i hedvábné, cikádami zvonicí noci, kdy tiše rostlo rozhořováním velikých Vašich hvězd a s rhytmickým harašením oblázků pod vlnami pobřeží, vidím celý ten Váš divoce krásný svět mezi zlatými věžemi Jalty a stoletými cedry Alupky, útesy pobřežních skal, podobných zkamenělé bouři země, háje sametových cypřišů a ojíněných oliv, z nichž bílé zámky svítí mramorem, tatarské chaty na stráních a prašné silnice, zvučící kavalkádami, pohoří borů, tmících se vysoko nad plamennou radostí břehu a zvedajících slavně k nebi a k jeho orlům bílý trůn Aj-Petri,

vzpomínám na jemnou laskavost Vašich dlaní, s jakou mi otevřely tento svět, na dobrotu Vašich očí, s jakou hleděly na zrání mého díla, vzpomínám na lásku a obdiv, jaké přinášíte touhám a konání všeho mého národa, na veškerou radost, kterou se s ním radujete ve dnech šťastných, i na bolest, jakou s ním trpíte ve dnech bloudění a smutku

a kladu s úctou i radostí do Vašich rukou, Paní, tuto knihu. Přijměte ji, prosím, jako skromný výraz hlubokých citů.

Dᴿ ARNOŠT DVOŘÁK

DEDICATION PAGE DESIGNED BY V. H. BRUNNER, FOR PUSHKIN'S "HISTORY OF THE CZAR SALTAN." PUBLISHED BY THE "SPOLEK ČESKÝCH BIBLIOFILŮ"

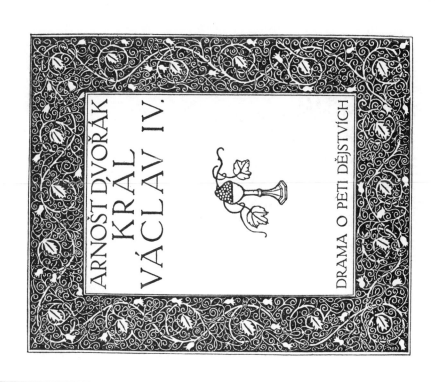

TITLE-PAGE DESIGNED BY F. KYSELA. PUBLISHED BY THE "NOVA EDICE," PRAGUE

TITLE-PAGE DESIGNED BY VLADIMÍR ŽUPANSKÝ. PUBLISHED BY
THE "SPOLEK MANES," PRAGUE

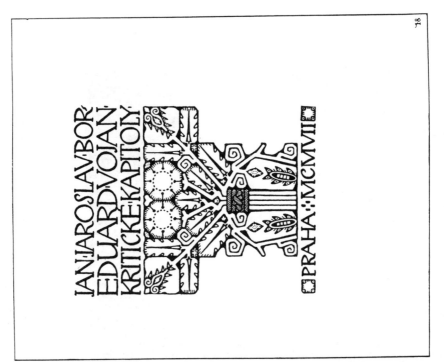

TITLE-PAGE DESIGNED BY J. BENDA. PUBLISHED BY
HEJDA A TUČEK, PRAGUE

Liber scriptus tum docetur
In quo tolum continetur
Undeo mudus iudicetur

Iudex ergo cum sedebit
Quidquid latet comparebit
Nil incultum remanebit

Quid sum miser tunc dicturus
Quem patronum rogaturus
Dum vix justus sit securus

Rex tremendae maiestalis
Qui salvandos salvas gratis
Salva me fons pietatis

Recordare Jesu pie
Quod sim causa tuae viae
Ne me perdas illa die

THOMAS
DE
CELANO

Dies irae, dies illa
Solvet saeclum cum favilla
Teste David cum Sybilla

Tantus tremor est futurus
Quando iudex est venturus
Cuncta stricte discussurus

Tuba mirum sparget sonum
Der sepulcra regionum
Cogens omnes ante thronum

Mens stupescit et natura
Cum resurgit creatura
Judicanti responsura

PAGES OF TYPE AND BORDER DESIGNED BY PROFESSOR
C. O. CZESCHKA, CAST BY GENZSCH AND HEYSE, HAMBURG

MINUSKEL
ANTIQUA~SCHRIFT
Es gibt nichts Unbedeu=
tendes in der Welt. Es
kommt nur auf die An=
schauungsweise an.-jp

vater unser/der du bist
im himmel/geheiliget wer=
de dein name/zukomme
uns dein reich/dein wille
geschehe wie im himmel
also auch auf erden. gib
uns heute unser tägliches
brot und vergib uns un=
sere schuld/wie auch wir
vergeben unseren schuld=
gern und führe uns nicht
in versuchung/sondern
erlöse uns von allem übel.

CURSID~SCHRIFT
BADEN Y WOLKE R
GMPDGFHZKJT
dampften ausgleichend/so y
jetzt wirkte box von quellen

EINLADUNG ZUR
FASTNACHTSKNEIDE
DES WR·AKAD· TURN=
VEREINES
AM 17. MÄRZ 1908
HOTEL BAYR·HOF
II·TABORSTRASSE
BEGINN ½9 UHR·
EINTRITT: 2 KRONEN
FAMILIEN: 3 PERS: 5K
STUDENTENKARTEN: 1K

BOOKBINDING IN BLACK SHAGREEN, WITH EMBOSSED GOLD ORNAMENTATION
DESIGNED BY RUDOLPH GEYER, EXECUTED BY ALBERT GÜNTHER

BOOKBINDING IN RED SHAGREEN, WITH EMBOSSED GOLD ORNAMENTATION
DESIGNED BY RUDOLPH GEYER, EXECUTED BY ALBERT GÜNTHER

BOOKBINDING IN RUSSIAN LEATHER, WITH INLAY AND TOOLING. DESIGNED
BY HENRYK UZIEMBLO, EXECUTED BY ROBERT JAHODA

BOOKBINDING IN RUSSIAN LEATHER, WITH INLAY AND TOOLING. DESIGNED
BY HENRYK UZIEMBLO, EXECUTED BY ROBERT JAHODA

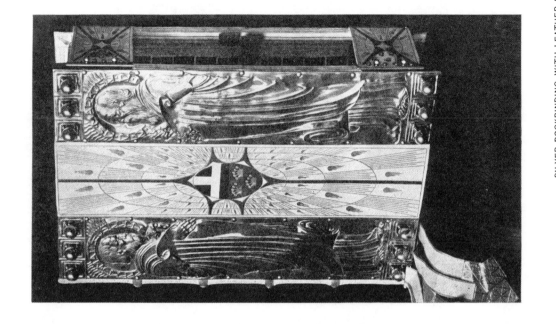

SILVER BOOKBINDING, WITH LEATHER INLAY AND
GOLD TOOLING. BY ANTON HOFER

(In the possession of H.E. Dr. Friedrich
Piffl, Prince-Bishop of Vienna)

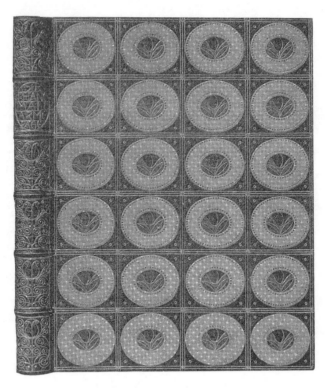

LEATHER BOOKBINDING, WITH INLAY AND GOLD
TOOLING. DESIGNED BY PROF. JOSEF HOFFMANN
EXECUTED BY THE WIENER WERKSTAETTE

BOOKBINDING IN BUCKSKIN, WITH INLAY AND TOOLING. DESIGNED BY PROF. JOSEF HOFFMANN
EXECUTED BY THE WIENER WERKSTAETTE

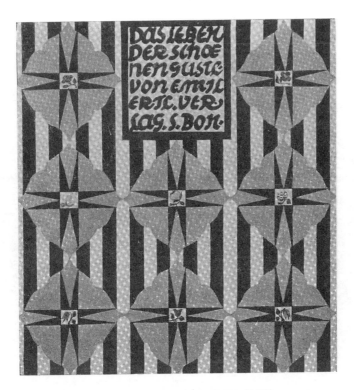

PAPER COVER DESIGNED BY DORA GROSS

PAPER COVER DESIGNED BY HANSI BURGER-DIVECKY, PRINTED IN
THE IMPERIAL GRAPHISCHE LEHR-UND-VERSUCHSANSTALT, VIENNA

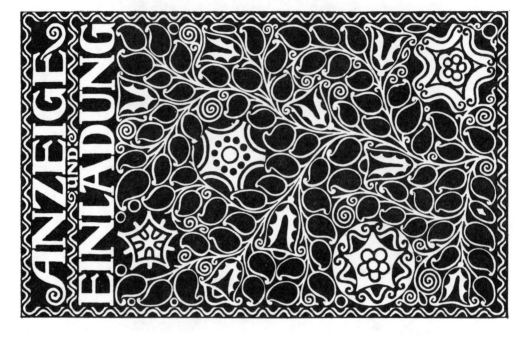

PAPER COVER DESIGNED BY
GUSTAV KALHAMMER

PAPER COVER DESIGNED BY ROBERT FUCHS, PRINTED IN THE
IMPERIAL GRAPHISCHE LEHR-UND-VERSUCHSANSTALT, VIENNA

228

PAPER COVER DESIGNED BY F. KOBLIHA

PAPER COVER DESIGNED BY ANTON HOFER.   FOR THEYER UND HARDTMUTH

TAILPIECE AND COVER DESIGN
BY HEDWIG SCHMIEDL

BORDER AND END-PAPER DESIGNS BY ALFRED
KELLER. FOR L. STAAKMANN, LEIPZIG

233

234

INITIAL LETTER AND BORDER DESIGNED BY PROF. C. O.
CZESCHKA. FOR GENZSCH AND HEYSE, HAMBURG

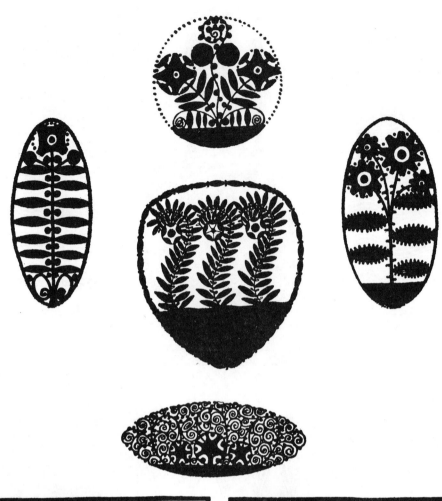

ORNAMENTS AND TAILPIECES BY WENZEL OSWALD

236

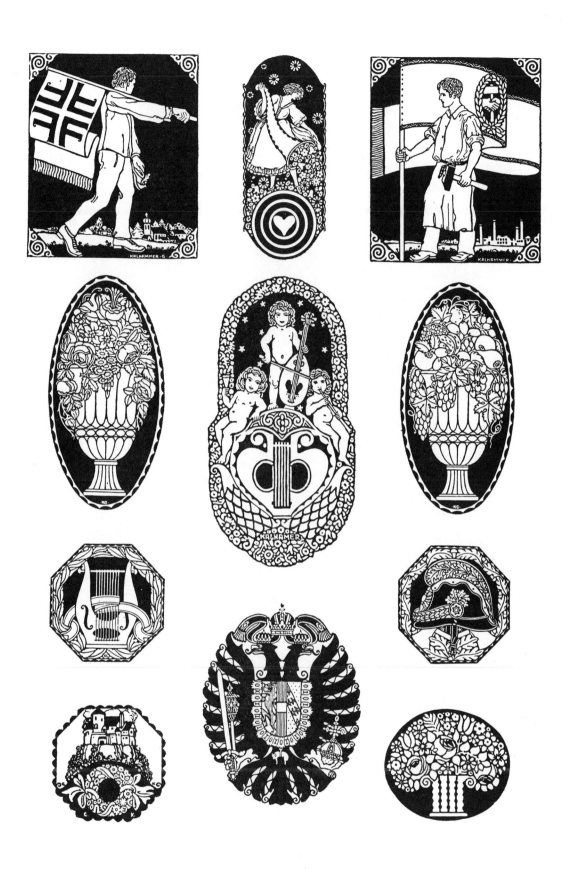

ORNAMENTS BY GUSTAV KALHAMMER

237

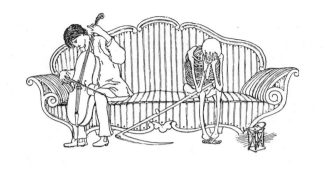

DECORATIVE ILLUSTRATIONS BY FERDINAND STAEGER

DECORATIVE ILLUSTRATIONS BY FERDINAND STAEGER

239

DECORATIVE ILLUSTRATIONS BY ALFRED KELLER, FOR
R. H. BARTSCH'S " BITTERSÜSSE LIEBESGESCHICHTE "
PUBLISHED BY L. STAAKMANN, LEIPZIG

240

DECORATIVE ILLUSTRATION BY ALFRED KELLER
FOR "DAS BUCH DER KLEINEN KLEINEN"
PUBLISHED BY L. STAAKMANN, LEIPZIG

DECORATIVE ILLUSTRATION BY
C. HASSELWANDER

DECORATIVE ILLUSTRATION BY C. KÖYSTRAND
FOR "PIERROT ALS SCHILDWACHE" PUB-
LISHED BY S. CZEIGER

INITIAL LETTER BY GUSTAV MARISCH

DECORATIVE ILLUSTRATIONS BY MARIANNE HITSCHMANN-STEINBERGER
FOR "KONEGEN'S KINDERBÜCHER." PUBLISHED BY KONEGEN, VIENNA

THE ART OF THE BOOK IN HUNGARY

THE development of art in Hungary reached its highest point in the fifteenth century. The influence of the Italian renaissance made itself felt in this country sooner than anywhere else, for Mathias Corvinus gathered round him at his Court a great many Italian artists and humanists, and acquired numerous finely painted books and manuscripts. The few remaining treasures of his library, called *corvinas*, are wonderful examples of renaissance book-illustrations, mostly the work of Italian miniaturists, for it would seem that Hungarian artists were not employed by the King. Political conflicts and wars put an end to the progress of art, and then came the domination of the Turks, who destroyed, or allowed to perish, the existing monuments of art. ✍ There are many reasons to account for the long period of depression in book-production and illustrative art which followed. Up to as late as the middle of the nineteenth century the educated classes in Hungary adopted Latin for conversation, and it was also the official and legal language of the country. Students went to Italy and Germany to acquire culture. Consequently foreign influences were paramount, and only the cheapest books were produced at home. The native typography could not compete with that of other countries, the art of the book fell into decay, and Hungarian artists were only employed in work of lesser importance. ✍ The books which have been published in Hungary during the last few years show a distinct advance when compared with those previously produced. This is in a large measure due to the training offered at the National Arts and Crafts School at Budapest, where opportunity is given for the study of typography, and characters based on the national art have been introduced and popularized. There is a special class for designing script based upon the best of the old national manuscripts which combine the most desirable qualities—legibility and artistic form. Three excellent examples of the work of the students are reproduced on pages 249 to 251. ✍ Hungary is happy in possessing a number of really clever book decorators, though many of them have settled outside their native country, and their work has in some respects little of the

TITLE-PAGE WRITTEN IN CORK. BY BLASIUS BUSAY (ARTS AND CRAFTS SCHOOL, BUDAPEST)

HEADPIECE AND INITIAL LETTER
BY ALEXANDER NAGY. PUBLISHED
BY THE "JÓKAI" PRINTING OFFICE

purely national characteristics. A notable example of this is to be found in the drawings of the Marquis Franz von Bayros, a Hungarian by race, Croatia being his native province, whose work bears no relation to his nationality. Delicate, refined, and eminently decorative, it possesses a grace which recalls the poetic charm of the *fêtes galantes*, and is yet, in its technical dexterity and subtle comprehension of the requirements of black-and-white, modern in feeling. We reproduce some charming examples of this artist's work. Very different in conception and treatment, but more national in character, is the decorative illustration by Charles Kós (page 248) for his poem, "The Death of Attila"; while other eminent book-decorators are Willy Pogány, many of whose drawings have been published in England, Alexander Nagy and Kriesch-Körösföi, both leaders of the famous Gödöllö group of artists. Nagy is a master of line, endowed with a poetic imagination, and he adopts with wonderful success those forms in which the Hungarian nation is so rich. Characteristic of his art is the headpiece shown on this page. A quaintly treated frontispiece by Blasius Busay is also reproduced. The original design was executed in burnt cork.

244

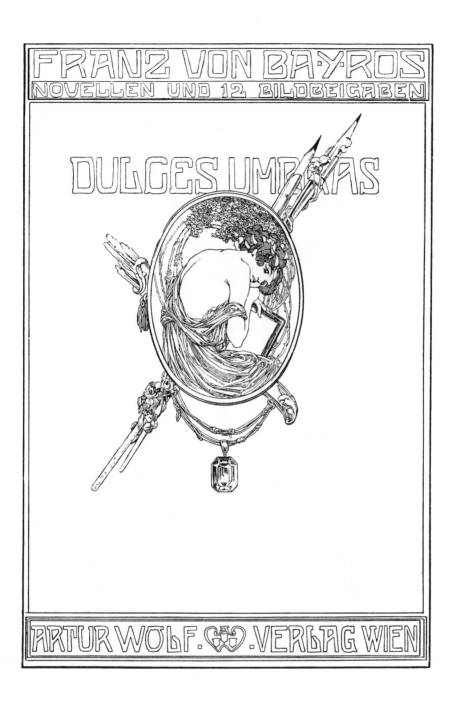

TITLE-PAGE DESIGNED BY FRANZ VON BAYROS
PUBLISHED BY ARTUR WOLF, VIENNA

DECORATIVE ILLUSTRATIONS BY FRANZ VON BAYROS
PUBLISHED BY ARTUR WOLF, VIENNA

BOOK-COVER DESIGN BY FRANZ VON BAYROS, FOR
L. H. ROSEGGER'S "VON KÖNIGEN UND JAKOBINERN"
PUBLISHED BY SEIFFERT, KOSTRITZ

DECORATIVE ILLUSTRATION BY FRANZ VON BAYROS
FOR VON SCHLOEMPS'S "DER PERVERSE MAIKÄFER"
PUBLISHED BY GEORG MÜLLER, MUNICH

247

"DEATH OF ATTILA."—DECORATIVE
ILLUSTRATION BY CHARLES KOS

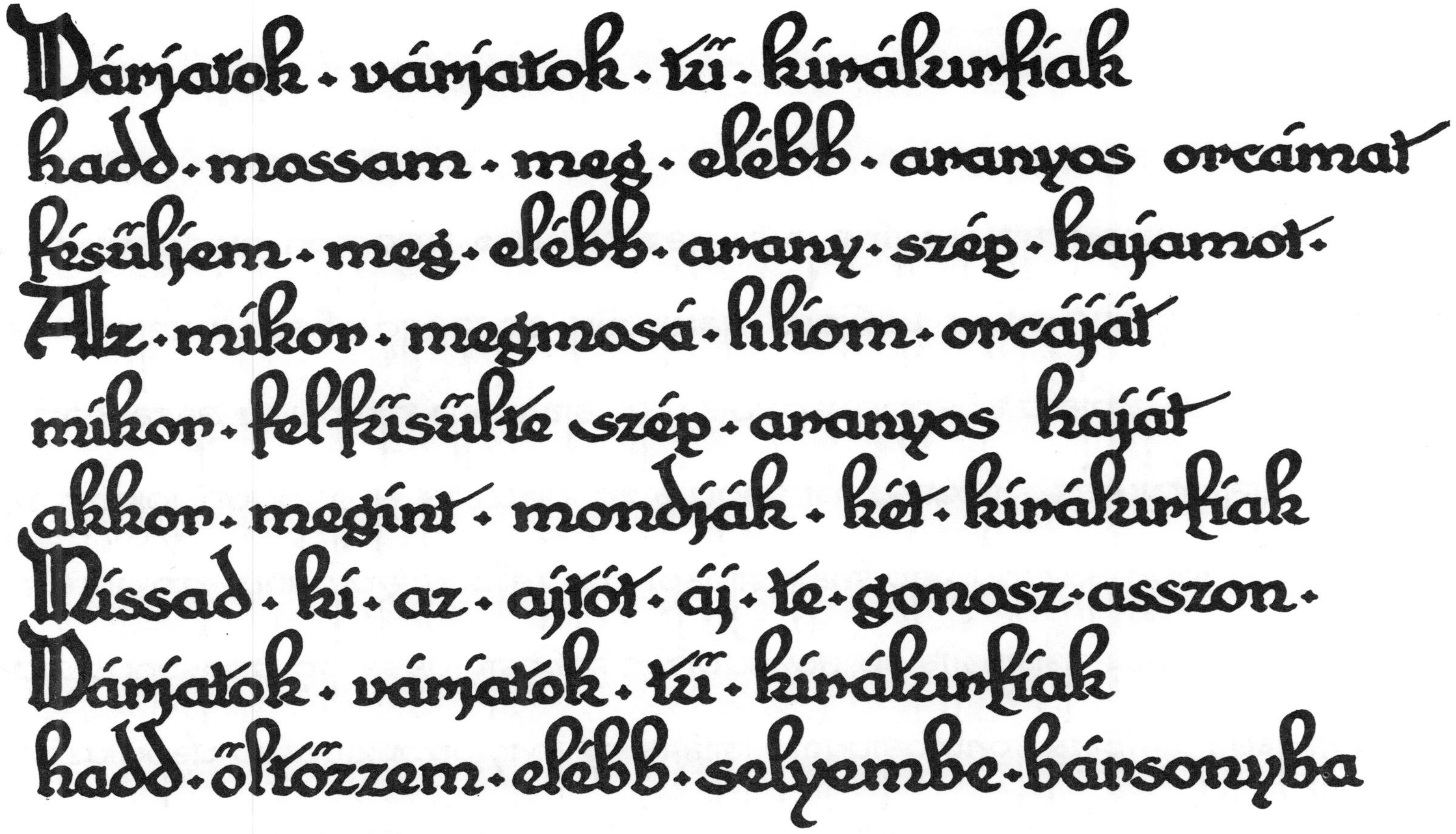

hogy mi a gyengébbel el akarjuk nyomni az erősebbel s hogy az emberi tár-

sadalom bizonyos csállapotál akarjuk előreszíteni, mely egy magasabb kul-

túra minden organizácziojaval és kifejlel technikajaval kiegyenlíthetellen el-

lenmondásban áll. és sajátságos, ugyanazok az ellenfelek, másik szavuk-

ba már azt mondják, hogy túlzo idealisztikus ábrandozók vagyunk, kik

oly utopiai gondolak ki, mely az emberi természettel semmiféleképen sem

egyez. ezek mind oly ellenvetések és okoskodasok, melyek roppant he-

ves szellemi megerőltelésbe kerülnek, melyek végelekig banalisok és

a melyek, ha valóban a mi nézeleinkkel sujlhalnak. Kalona Imre.

EXAMPLE OF WRITING WITH REED PEN. BY IMRE KATONA
STUDENT OF THE ARTS AND CRAFTS SCHOOL, BUDAPEST

Az anarkia kivihetősége. dr. Schmitt Jenő-től:

Teljesen hihetetlen ama nézetek felületessége, melyek az ellenséges táborban, s ez az egész világ, az anarkia kivihetőségére vonatkozólag uralkodnak s hihetetlen durvák az ellenérvek, melyekkel tisztán az elv ellen fölhoznak. Tudósok, tudatlanok egyiránt használják ezt a durva érvelést és nyugodtan mondhatjuk hogy soha nagyobb dolgot noha volt reá alkalom nyomorúságosabb fegyverekkel megnem támadtak. Amit legelőször is léptennyomon szemünkre lobbantanak, az az ellenvetés, hogy ha a központi erőszakuralmat megszüntetjük, akkor szabad a vásár rablóknak, lotvajoknak, utonállóknak, azután hogy az anarkia győzelmével zürzavar állana be. Katona Imre.

EXAMPLE OF WRITING WITH REED PEN. BY IMRE KATONA
STUDENT OF THE ARTS AND CRAFTS SCHOOL, BUDAPEST

ORNAMENT BY FRANZ VON BAYROS, FOR "DIE
SECHZEHNTE EHEFREUDE." PUBLISHED BY
ARTUR WOLF, VIENNA

252

SWEDEN

THE ART OF THE BOOK IN SWEDEN
BY AUGUST BRUNIUS

IN Sweden, as elsewhere, the latter half of the nineteenth century brought about a brighter period for the Art of the Book as regards typography, quality of paper, and binding. Still the decay had hardly been as great as in other branches of decoration and handicraft. Two publishing firms, P. A. Norstedt, Stockholm, and Berling, Lund, have maintained a high standard of bookmaking. On the other hand, a more artistic character was adopted between 1870 and 1880 by using traditional means, by imitating Gothic manuscripts, or by a somewhat arbitrary use of Old Northern ornamental art. The renaissance, which in Sweden burst forth at the beginning of the nineties, originated in a revival of interest in the decorative arts, especially in the textiles of the Viking and Saga periods. The Old Northern spirit ran like an undercurrent through the life of the whole country, and culminated in Artur Hazelius's epoch-making museum work, Skansen and the Northern Museum. Just at the right moment there was added a practical study of modern bookmaking in England and on the Continent. A whole generation was seized by the new ideas which were proclaimed with such power by William Morris. To initiate a movement, combining as it does artistic and practical knowledge, a passionate idealist is required. Such an idealist is Waldemar Zachrisson, a printer of Gothenburg (born 1861). He studied in Sweden and at the best printing firms in Hamburg, Leipzig, Vienna, Berlin, and St. Petersburg, and developed his taste by constant study of the masterpieces of great times and the new English and American fine printing practised by Morris and De Vinne. As soon as he had secured his own great business he began to work for the raising of the whole trade. He founded a union of experts, "Allmänna Svenska Boktrycka-

PAGE FROM "A HISTORY OF SWEDISH WOODCUTS." ORNAMENTS BY ARTUR SAHLÉN. PRINTED BY NORSTEDT UND SÖNER

255

reföreningen " (Swedish Printers' Society), which worked for the establishment of the Museum of Industrial Art in Stockholm and the Technical School for Industrial Art in Gothenburg. In a number of ways, through artistic advertisements and articles in the trade papers, he tried to prepare the ground for a higher standard in the printing-trade generally, and his distinct practical outlook made his efforts eminently successful. ⚜ Lately in Sweden the common feature in the aims for developing the art of the book has been the accentuation of the national character. The difficulties have here been considerable. As yet we do not possess a fount designed by a Swedish artist, but the types we have are founded on an old predilection for the Roman type. Already in 1550 the Roman type had been introduced into Sweden. During the seventeenth and eighteenth centuries Swedish taste was concentrated upon Dutch and French models. The Roman type which is now used in Sweden, and which is cut in Hamburg, suggests Caslon's somewhat modernized type. It is called " Mediæval-Roman," and has many advantages, is easy to read, and has an unassuming simplicity. The light tone may perhaps sometimes seem monotonously grey. English readers will certainly find its resemblance to the English type, but will also easily discover the differences. ⚜ It is characteristic of Swedish printing that it appears to best advantage and is most personal in publications of an occasional character intended for a select public. The rest of the productions are on a considerably lower level. To English and French tastes our *belles lettres* show an astonishing lack of typographical unity. There is a great variety in the size and make-up, and also various many-coloured paper covers, both of good and bad style, are used. However, an improvement has occurred in the last few years, a quieter taste has manifested itself. A good step forward is the excellent publication of Swedish classics issued by the " Svenska Vitterhetssamfundet " (the Swedish Literature Society), and printed at Albert Bonnier's works. Here a severe and pure style is combined with exquisite material, and great care is bestowed upon the typography. An undertaking like this would be a credit to any country. In equally good style is the Swedish edition of Olaus Magnus's " Historia de Gentibus Septentrionalibus," published by another society, the " Michaelisgillet " (the Michael Guild). It was written about 1550 by the last Catholic Archbishop of Sweden, who was one of the greatest travellers and most interesting writers of the Renaissance. The text is illustrated by old woodcuts, which had been carried out according to Olaus Magnus's own designs. Two volumes of this splendid work have been printed by Almqvist and Wiksell, Uppsala. ⚜ In a similar manner the great Handicraft Exhibition at Stockholm in 1909 produced four Swedish classics ; they were given as prizes in a lottery. These four books were arranged and

256

printed by four different firms, an achievement which could not have been accomplished ten years earlier. ✠ This general survey of the art of the book during the last decades would be incomplete if it did not mention a printing firm which, through its good typography, now occupies a prominent position. The two brothers Hugo and Carl Lagerström have bestowed a great deal of labour on trying to attain a higher level in printing. They learnt their trade in Germany, England, and France, and worked for some years—one in Stockholm, the other in Copenhagen—before they founded the Lagerström Brothers printing firm in 1903. They have also taken a prominent part in the arts and crafts movement generally. They started a paper called the *Nordisk Boktryckarkonst* (Northern Art of Printing), and founded two societies, one of which is the abovementioned "Michaelisgillet." Dr. Isak Collijn, a distinguished librarian, was the third founder. ✠ The first book Lagerström Brothers printed was a kind of typographical prospectus. Among the eight volumes by August Strindberg there is a chemical work called "Antibarbarus." This book was decorated by a young artist, Artur Sjögren, who is a book-decorator with a profound knowledge of old Swedish typography. The book was printed in a small choice edition on hand-made paper, and four pages are shown here (pp. 157 to 160). Since then Lagerström Brothers have published numerous large and small books, always for a more limited public, but at a price which only slightly exceeds the ordinary book-prices. Their productions express the same ideas of compromise that the English Medici Society is striving for. ✠ The bibliophile public in Sweden leans towards the old books, and would not support a real aristocratic book - business on new lines and with modern aims. Lagerström Brothers, however, have printed some of the most beautiful Swedish books, with and without decoration : a couple of historical memoirs from the time of Charles XII; a series of small

FÖRTAALET ELLER INGÅNG:

EEN ALLMENNELIGH PRACTICA ELLER VÄDER-BOOK/ EFFTER THE GAMBLE OCH VIJSE ALBERTI, ALKINDI, HALI, OCH PTOLOMEI LÄR-DOM/ STÄDZE VARANDES ÅHR IFRÅ ÅHR

DET ÄR ITT VIST OCH SANT ORDSPRÅK som allmeent säyes: Dhet är een godh Vän som varaar een annan för Olyckan och Skadan för än den kommer. Therföre är een gladh och godh tiende väl värd/ at man henne förkunnar. Effter thet alla Practikor och Prophetier/ icke allenast äre skriffne aff then Helge Andes uppenbarelse/ uthan och andre/ hvilket een part eendels aff lång Himmelens Lopp/ aff Planeternes och andra Stiernors beskådelse/ och een part eendels aff lång Förfahrenheet/ aff Himmelens Täckn och många Omständigheeter äre uthdragne och begrundade/ äre ther förordnat och i värcket stälte/ at vij dher aff om Lycko och olycko om/ Väder och Oväder tilförenne eller framföre åth medh goda tiender och sann Budhskap undervijste/ skulle värnade varda/ och så städze och altijdh om Lycko och Olycko förorsakas at fruchta och troo den alzmächtige gode Gudh.

¸Så är thet rätt och tilbörligit/ ja Christeligh Kärleek och Plicht fordrar thet ock så medh sigh/ at man gladeligh och medh Tacksäyelse anammar alla Praktiker och Prophetier/ som äre genom then H. Anda tillkenna giffne/ jemväl aff androm/ både konstrijke naturlige Stiernokikare/ och andre

7

PAGE FROM "BONDE-PRACTICA." INITIAL LETTER BY LEON WELAMSON. PRINTED BY BRÖDERNA-LAGERSTRÖM

257

books selected from old Swedish literature ; and finally, a reprint of a book which certainly has no equivalent in English literature, but which all the same would probably have some interest for an English public. The title is "Bonde-practica," and it is a kind of text-book for peasants in nature-study and hygiene, partly written in verse. The book was published for the first time in 1662. It is a collection of observations founded on the theories of astrology, and told with much humour. This book reveals the Swedish outlook on life and the education of the people in olden times. Leon Welamson, a young artist, has made for the new edition of this curious old book some simple and vigorous illustrations, which without being imitations are executed in the old style. It is a masterpiece of Swedish typography. ⚜ Book illustrations and decoration play an important part in the modern art of the book. Illustrated books have always been popular, and many of our best artists of to-day began their careers as illustrators. Carl Larsson is a typical Swedish illustrator and a distinguished painter. He illustrates, in colour or black-and-white, his own text. But he belongs to an older school in so far as he does not pay so much attention to the claims of decoration. Olle Hjortzberg is a comparatively young artist. He is in part influenced by the modern English school of book decorators, and has done work that would satisfy even the most exacting critics. He has acquired an extraordinary mastery over the early Christian language of symbols, and has in his books used it in an ornamental manner with great success. At present he is engaged on a richly decorated "State" Bible, ("Gustav V's Bible,") a gigantic undertaking, in which both artist and printer hope to surpass themselves (p. 260). ⚜ While Olle Hjortzberg and Artur Sjögren are more closely attached to the technique of the book, Einar Nerman, one of the youngest Swedish artists, is more independent. He has illustrated several children's books and has done some caricatures. There is a touch of the rococo in his drawing, and elegance combined with a bold wit which proves some French influence. His curving lines bring forth a "roguishness" that is unparalleled in Swedish art, and can compare with the best foreign

examples. The illustrations to the well-known tale by Hans Andersen, "Peter the Swineherd" (p. 264), are purely original. ❧ Finally, a few words regarding modern Swedish bookbinding. Our productions have, from the sixteenth century up to the present time, followed sometimes German and sometimes French models; during certain periods, however, our craftsman have produced work important and original enough to be called "Swedish." The middle of the eighteenth century especially was a flourishing age for the art of bookbinding. A hundred years later the art began to lose its value and importance, but before many decades had passed the first sign of an upward tendency was noticed. It was in 1886, when Gustaf Hedberg returned from Paris and London where he had been studying for a long time. He has designed and carried out numerous bindings, and has been especially successful in attaining a rich effect by small means. His ingenuity and ability in giving even to a simple binding an original character are qualities associated with the great craftsmen of all time. ❧ The Countess Eva Sparre, *née* Mannerheim, is at present our leading artist in bookbinding, in the sense that the work is entirely her own, independent of traditional style and original in composition, in execution, and especially in colour-effects. She has not executed a great number of bindings, but they are all distinguished by individual character, very modest in their ornamentation, and exquisite in the use of the materials. Miss Greta Morssing, who has chiefly studied the modern English tooled work, is also an accomplished exponent of the art.

INITIAL LETTERS DESIGNED BY ARTUR SJÖGREN

GENESIS
FÖRSTA
MOSE
BOK

HALF-TITLE PAGE FROM GUSTAV V'S BIBLE. DESIGNED BY
OLLE HJORTZBERG, PRINTED BY BRÖDERNA LAGERSTRÖM

BOOKBINDING IN NIGER MOROCCO, WITH INLAY
AND GOLD TOOLING. BY GRETA MORSSING

BOOKBINDING IN NIGER MOROCCO, WITH INLAY
AND GOLD TOOLING. BY GRETA MORSSING

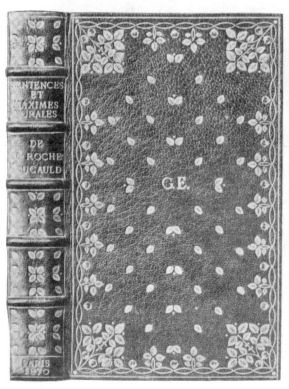

BOOKBINDING IN RED MOROCCO, WITH INLAY
AND GOLD TOOLING. BY GRETA MORSSING

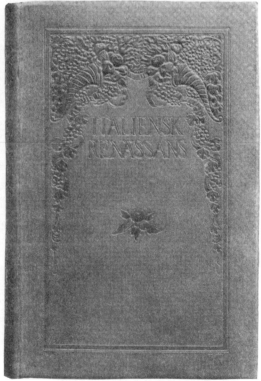

BOOKBINDING IN TOOLED LEATHER
BY COUNTESS EVA SPARRE

261

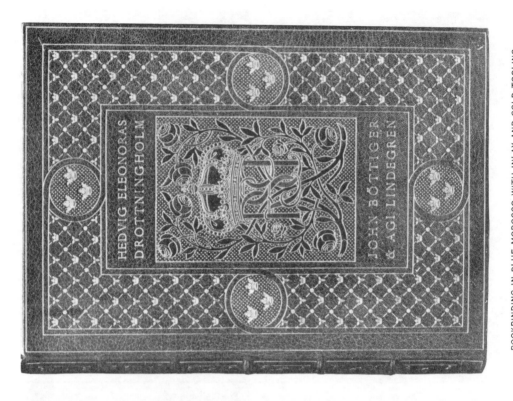

BOOKBINDING IN BLUE MOROCCO, WITH INLAY AND GOLD TOOLING
BY GUSTAF HEDBERG

BOOKBINDING IN RED CALF, WITH GOLD TOOLING
BY GUSTAF HEDBERG

262

BOOKBINDING IN BROWN MOROCCO, WITH INLAY AND GOLD TOOLING
BY GUSTAF HEDBERG

BOOKBINDING IN GREEN MOROCCO, WITH GOLD TOOLING
BY GUSTAF HEDBERG

HEADPIECES BY EINAR NERMAN FOR HANS
ANDERSEN'S "PER SVINAHERDE," PUBLISHED
BY P. A. NORSTEDT UND SÖNER

AMERICA

THE ART OF THE BOOK IN AMERICA
BY WILLIAM DANA ORCUTT

THE Art of the Book in America received a tremendous impetus as a result of the work of William Morris in England. Previous to that time American printing showed no originality, the finest examples being based firmly upon the best English work of the period. The highest point of excellence was reached during the decade from 1860 to 1870, and no better example of orthodox printing could be cited than the " Life of Prescott," produced by the University Press in 1864. After 1870, and down to the date of the Morris revival, well-made volumes were issued from the University, the Riverside and the De Vinne Presses, but the average quality deteriorated. The transition of book-making from a trade to an art dates from the appearance of the Kelmscott volumes. ✎ Naturally enough, the early effect of the enthusiasm over Morris's work was the issuance of a series of monstrosities ; but the very mistakes made by these zealous typographical disciples were educational, producing a momentum which finally brought excellent results. Those who copied Morris failed ; those who were encouraged by his departure from the beaten track to think for themselves succeeded in retaining the basic principles upon which the work of the master printers has always firmly rested, applying them in the light of modern conditions, and giving them originality by their individual experiments. Morris's work made men think, broke down the smugness of precedent, and enabled printing to become an art. ✎ Cobden-Sanderson's work accomplished much in helping American printing to assume a sane status after the hectic enthusiasm of the Morris period. Students of typography came to realize that William Morris belonged to the great decorators rather than to the master printers ; that it was his superb presswork, and the general harmony of the factors which went into his books, rather than his typography overloaded with design, which represented his real contribution to the making of the Book Ideal. When the Doves Press, in continuing Morris's work, substituted a more classical fount of type, based upon an Italian model of the fifteenth century, there was a quick response in America in dropping the tendency towards the Gothic, engendered by the type faces cut by the Kelmscott Press. During the next ten years more original and better types were cut, and volumes were produced which carried printing as an art to a higher point than it had previously attained. ✎ Of the types cut under the so-called Gothic influence, the " Renner " of the De Vinne Press is among the best. Theodore L. De Vinne, whose recent death removed the *doyen* of American master printers, was responsible for the well-sustained reputation of his Press during his active association with it. As a technical master of typography, and in his magnificent presswork, he translated himself into his books, but the exactness of his training is reproduced in his translation of Renner's design into the rigidity of modern type. The page which is reproduced here (p. 272), taken from one of the many superb Grolier Club publications produced by the De Vinne Press, shows both the Renner model and the modern expression of it as interpreted by Mr. De Vinne. The oblique serif of the *e*, the fancy curve to the *h*, and the superfluous curl at the top of the *g* introduce features which are foreign to the model, and give to the modern type a "jobbiness" which unquestionably detracts from the otherwise dignified appearance of the face. ✠ The Gilliss Press, whose work is now suspended, has contributed its share to the renaissance of printing in America. Its limited editions of the books of William Loring Andrews and other volumes issued for private distribution show excellence of workmanship and harmony in conception rather than originality in treatment. Instead of specially designed type, these volumes are rich in decoration, the artistic quality of which ranks with the best. ✠ At the Merrymount Press, Mr. D. Berkeley Updike has produced a number of volumes which have made their impress upon American typography because of his sincerity in carrying out his announced purpose of "undertaking the work of to-day in the spirit of the best days of printing." Two special faces of type have been designed for the Merrymount Press, both of which are among the successful faces cut in America. The "Montallegro" type, designed by Herbert P. Horne, of London, is used in the volumes of the "Humanistic Library," issued by Mr. Updike, of which a page is here given (p. 273). Of the type the London *Athenæum* says: "We are inclined to say not only that it is better than any of the many attempts which have resulted from Morris's revival of the art of printing, but also that it is even more perfect than any of the fifteenth-century founts on the study of which that revival was based. It is . . . absolutely without affectation . . . and so perfectly are the proportions of the letters harmonized that every page is a thing of beauty. We regret that it was reserved for an American printer to bring out such an admirable fount. . . . It is the first time that a fount has been designed in modern times which satisfies at once practical and æsthetic demands. Mr. Horne has solved a problem which has exercised us ever since we began to think again that printing was an art." ✠ The "Merrymount" type, designed by Bertram Grosvenor Goodhue, is based upon fifteenth-century models, and has attracted much favourable comment. The "Holy Bible" and the "Life of Benvenuto Cellini," from which pages are here reproduced (p. 277), are representative examples both of the type and of the typographical standards of the Press. ✠ The writer of this present article would hesitate to include his own design of "Humanistic" type except that it has come to be accepted by typographical students as representing an approach to the art from a standpoint entirely different from that of other designers. The first types were naturally based upon the best hand-lettering of their time, yet hand-lettering, as an art, reached its zenith after printing began, in the work of the Humanistic scribes. This type is based therefore not upon an early type, but upon hand-lettering at its highest point of perfection. The pages which are shown here (pp. 274 and 275) have been taken from "The Triumphs of Francesco Petrarch," produced at the University Press under the writer's supervision. An examination of these pages will show that the principle upon which the fount is cut differs radically from that shown in regular modern types, namely, the ascending letters are short and the descending letters long. The designs of the letters closely follow those of the handwritten model, yet avoid the inevitable slight irregularity of such work, which would prove unpleasant in a printed page. Instead of a single character for each letter, a certain variety is introduced by having several characters, the compositor being trained to use the different forms exactly as the hand would automatically make a change in hand-lettering. Charles Eliot Norton says of this : " Most modern type lacks freshness and individuality, and the new fount to which the name 'Humanistic' has been given shows its contrast to the familiar dry, mechanical form. There is attractive freedom and unusual grace in its lines, derived immediately from the manuscript model, but adapted to the necessary rigid requirements of print." ❧ Among other important volumes produced at the University Press are those decorated by Bertram Grosvenor Goodhue and Will Bradley, two artists whose work in book-decoration stands in a class by itself. Much of Goodhue's work reflects the Morris influence, as will be seen in the page shown from "Esther" (p. 276); but his ability in original design is indicated by the border and initial of the " Songs of Heredia," which is given on the same page. ❧ Bradley's work evidences the greatest versatility of any decorative artist America has produced. Some of his work shows Beardsley's influence, but no single influence could control so original a genius as Bradley has proved himself to be. The two examples reproduced here (pp. 278 and 279) represent the extremes in his work—one drawn with a delicacy and accuracy of line which is marvellous in its execution ; the other bold and heavy, giving a woodcut effect. ❧ No one artist-printer has contributed so much to American typography as Bruce Rogers, whose " Montaigne " type is easily the best and most practical of any special face, and whose productions while associated with the Riverside Press are marked by an originality and a consistency of excellence beyond what has been attained by any other

American printer. He, better than anyone else, through his knowledge of types and his skill as a designer, has given expression to the basic principles of the old-time master printers awakened by modern conditions. His monumental folio edition of Montaigne—pages of which are reproduced here (pp. 280 and 281)—demonstrates a harmony of effect eminently appropriate to the style and period of its contents. The type itself is based upon an early French model, and the decorations and the initial letters (p. 282) are free renderings by Rogers of the original designs by Tory, in which the retention of the designer's spirit is admirably accomplished. ✠ During the past five years the Plimpton Press has contributed much to elevate the standard of printing and binding by abolishing to a large extent the prevalent custom of publishers to produce their volumes by " piecemeal." This has resulted in changing the making of books from a contracting to a manufacturing business, and has had its effect in raising the quality of the so-called " trade " volumes. When the composition, presswork, and binding of a book are divided up among as many firms, the result of the divided responsibility often means a general deterioration of quality ; but by the " complete manufacture " method the volume is planned out in advance, even to the paper, cover design, and illustrations, by a single mind. This places the printer in the position of expert manufacturing man to a large number of his customers, and enables him to preserve standards and to introduce economies by purchasing supplies in larger quantities, and by combining forms of text and illustrations in the manufacture. ✠ The influence which a publisher can exert upon the Art of the Book is shown by the series of classics issued in exquisite form by Mr. Thomas B. Mosher, at prices within the reach of all. These volumes are distinct evidences of his own taste and knowledge rather than triumphs of the printer, for Mr. Mosher has expressed himself in the type, margins, paper, and the general format of his admirable publications. ✠ It would be difficult to estimate the far-reaching results in the general advance in typographical standards due to two magazines, *The Printing Art* and *The Graphic Arts*. The monthly issues of these publications have shown ordinary printers how to produce work above the average by placing before them actual examples of the best combinations of type, paper, and colour harmonies. They have been educational in the extreme, teaching buyers of printing as well as printers how to secure the effects desired. ✠ In the matter of domestic production America shows little originality in book-papers, the " Old Stratford " being the only distinctive exception. No hand-made book-paper is now produced in America, owing principally to the high cost of labour. This makes it possible to import from England, France, and Italy cheaper than to manufacture at home. The " Old Stratford " paper,

270

however, is a unique product, and is used much in volumes of *de luxe* format, and in books where lasting qualities are demanded. In cover-papers, on the other hand, America produces a bewildering line, which quite excels those of other countries, offering a variety of selection which is a tremendous aid to the printer in securing artistic results. ✠ Fine bookbinding in America is at present confined to a small number of individual workers, mostly pupils of the famous English and French binders, and their principal claim to originality of processes may be said to be an effort to combine the workmanship of the English with the artistic skill in decoration of the French. The Club Bindery, which flourished in New York during the lifetime of Mr. Robert Hoe, could scarcely be called an American institution, as its best workmen were brought to this country for this special purpose. Since his death this bindery has been broken up, and the finest work is to-day being done by women. Their skill and workmanship rank high, but they are handicapped by the excessive cost of labour and by the fact that all their leathers must be imported. The inevitable higher price makes it natural that American book-collectors should continue to send their volumes abroad for fine bindings. Amongst those whose work is most highly prized may be mentioned Miss Sears and Miss St. John of Boston, and Miss Lahey of New York. ✠ In ordinary trade bindings the processes are more and more reduced to machine production, but in the best binderies this standardization has by no means proved a deterioration in quality. American trade books as a whole compare favourably with those of other countries, but it is quite true that the constantly increasing cost of every phase of book manufacture is in some instances causing American publishers to economize, and to accept a grade of work inferior to what they would have considered a few years ago. This, however, should not be regarded as a reflection upon American workmanship, but rather upon American conditions which force it. In cover design plain lettering still obtains for books of fiction and for serious works, but considerable elaboration is used upon smaller volumes issued as seasonable publications, or with a specific appeal. A few characteristic examples are reproduced on pp. 283 and 284. ✠ It is impossible, within the scope of this article, to do more than chronicle some of the results of the remarkable advance made in the standards of book-manufacturing in America during the past ten years. The knowledge of what constitutes a well-made volume is much greater than ever before, and the ability of the buying public to discriminate is the most hopeful promise for the future. In the omission of other examples of printing and binding, and of mention of other artists entitled to credit for the part they have played in advancing the Art of the Book in America, the writer pleads the limitations imposed by space.

and set his colophon entirely in capital letters. To call attention to the information in this colophon he put a broad blank between each line so that the composition should have a proper relief of white space and be made more readable.

Here it may be remarked that Jenson's beautiful roman type could be used to advantage only in large and high-priced books which were slow of sale. To insure a readier sale for subsequent books he, and Franz Renner too, had to print them upon new types,

Note
8

Rubertus celeber finxit non parua minorum
Gloria me fratrum Paulo regnante fecūdo.
Quarto fed Sixto ueniēs Halbrūna alemānus
Francifcus formis ueneta me preffit in urbe
Mille quadringentis & feptuaginta duobus .

From a book by Roberto de Litio. Franz Renner, Venice, 1472.

much smaller in size, and of the condensed gothic face or style then in favor as the only proper character for service books of devotion or of theology.

There were many printers in Italy during the last quarter of the fifteenth century who were not content with the mean position and scant wording of the traditional colophon. Some of them tried to vary the usual form of words, and to make the colophon more attractive by putting it in metre. Franz Renner and the brothers Speyer of Venice, Ulric Hahn of Rome, and others gave to the reader colophons in metre that call for merciful criticism. They did their best.

PAGE FROM "TITLE-PAGES" (THE GROLIER CLUB) PRINTED IN
THE "RENNER" TYPE DESIGNED BY THEODORE LOW DE VINNE

II
THOUGHTS ON ART

* *
*

HE painter's work will be of lit- Paint-
tle merit if he takes the paint- ing
ing of others as his standard, de-
but if he studies from nature clines
he will produce good fruits; as when
is seen in the case of the paint- aloof
ers of the age after the Romans, who continued to Na-
imitate one another and whose art consequently ture
declined from age to age. After these came Giotto
the Florentine, who was born in the lonely mountains, inhabited only by goats and similar animals; and he, being drawn to his art by nature,
began to draw on the rocks the doings of the
goats of which he was the keeper; and thus he
likewise began to draw all the animals which he
met with in the country: so that after long study
he surpassed not only all the masters of his age,
but all those of many past centuries. After him
art relapsed once more, because all artists imi-
tated the painted pictures, and thus from century to century it went on declining, until Tomaso
the Florentine, called Masaccio, proved by his
perfect work that they who set up for themselves a standard other than nature, the mistress
of all masters, labour in vain.

59

MERRYMOUNT PRESS: PAGE FROM "THE HUMANISTIC LIBRARY" PRINTED
IN THE "MONTALLEGRO" TYPE DESIGNED BY HERBERT P. HORNE

THE TRIUMPHS OF FRANCESCO PETRARCH

FLORENTINE POET LAUREATE
TRANSLATED BY HENRY BOYD
WITH AN INTRODUCTION
BY DOCTOR GUIDO BIAGI
LIBRARIAN OF THE
ROYAL MEDICEAN
LAURENTIAN LIBRARY
FLORENCE

IMPRINTED FOR LITTLE BROWN AND
COMPANY BOSTON MASSACHUSETTS
BY THE UNIVERSITY PRESS CAMBRIDGE U·S·A·

TITLE-PAGE FROM "THE TRIUMPHS OF FRANCESCO PETRARCH" (LITTLE,
BROWN AND CO. AND JOHN MURRAY) PRINTED IN THE "HUMANISTIC"
TYPE DESIGNED BY WILLIAM DANA ORCUTT

HERE AUSPICIOUSLY BEGINNETH
THE TRIUMPH OF LOVE
BY FRANCESCO PETRARCH
FLORENTINE POET LAUREATE

PART ONE OF THE TRIUMPH OF LOVE

Nel tempo che rinnova i miei sospiri

THE FATAL MORN
ING DAWN'D THAT
BROUGHT AGAIN* THE
SAD MEMORIAL OF
MY ANCIENT PAIN

That day, the source of long-protracted woe',
When I began the plagues of Love to know,

Hyperion's throne, along the azure field,
Between the splendid horns of Taurus wheel'd;

And from her spouse the Queen of Morn withdrew
Her sandals, gemm'd with frost-bespangled dew.

Sad recollection, rising with the morn,
Of my disastrous love, repaid with scorn,

---

* The anniversary of April 6, when his passion for Laura commenced.

PAGE FROM "THE TRIUMPHS OF FRANCESCO PETRARCH" (LITTLE,
BROWN AND CO. AND JOHN MURRAY) PRINTED IN THE "HUMANISTIC"
TYPE DESIGNED BY WILLIAM DANA ORCUTT

BORDER AND INITIAL LETTER DESIGNED BY BERTRAM GROSVENOR GOODHUE FOR "SONGS OF HEREDIA" (SMALL, MAYNARD AND CO.)

BORDER AND INITIAL LETTERS DESIGNED BY BERTRAM GROSVENOR GOODHUE FOR "ESTHER" (COPELAND AND DAY)

THE HOLY BIBLE

CONTAINING

THE OLD AND NEW TESTAMENTS

AND THE APOCRYPHA

III

JOSHUA, JUDGES, RUTH

AND

THE FIRST BOOK OF SAMUEL

R. H. HINKLEY COMPANY

BOSTON

THE LIFE OF

BENVENUTO CELLINI

BOOK FIRST

I

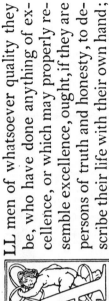 LL men of whatsoever quality they be, who have done anything of excellence, or which may properly resemble excellence, ought, if they are persons of truth and honesty, to describe their life with their own hand; but they ought not to attempt so fine an enterprise till they have passed the age of forty. This duty occurs to my own mind, now that I am travelling beyond the term of fifty-eight years, and am in Florence, the city of my birth. Many untoward things can I remember, such as happen to all who live upon our earth; and from those adversities I am now more free than at any previous period of my career—nay, it seems to me that I enjoy greater content of soul and health of body than ever I did in bygone years. I can also bring to mind some pleasant goods and some inestimable evils, which, when I turn my thoughts backward, strike terror in me, and astonishment that I should have reached this age of fifty-eight, wherein, thanks be to God, I am still travelling prosperously forward.

II

It is true that men who have laboured with some show of excellence, have already given knowledge

[71]

MERRYMOUNT PRESS: TITLE AND OPENING PAGES PRINTED IN THE "MERRYMOUNT" TYPE DESIGNED BY BERTRAM GROSVENOR GOODHUE

ANDREW CAMPBELL

TO fully appreciate the extent of the services rendered by Andrew Campbell, founder of the Campbell Company, to the printing art, it is only necessary to imagine for a moment what the present state of that art would be were it not for two, at least, of the many inventions and devices of which he was the originator. The Two-Revolution Press and the use of "hard packing" are due entirely to his ingenuity. It was Andrew Campbell who, impressed by the idea that speed, as well as impressional power, might be made a concomitant of a Cylinder Press, invented the "two-revolution" machine, the principle of which is now in such universal use that the class has become the standard one of the world. It was Andrew Campbell, again, who conceived the idea that a better result could be obtained if to the printing surface were opposed a hard in place of a soft and yielding packing. To put this revolutionary idea into effect necessitated the strengthening of the machine to such an extent as to enable it to adequately withstand the increased pressure requisite, and to build a machine of this nature cost Campbell a hard struggle and the work of a number of years. Eventually, however, he was victorious; and as a result the rubber blanket and the felt sheet are to-day confined to use upon newspaper presses alone. But these, though the chief, are not the only advantages the printing trade owes to Andrew Campbell. It was he, for instance, who invented the front fly delivery and was the first to deliver the printed sheet in such a fashion as to obviate the possibility of the freshly inked surface coming into contact with any part of the machine.

Of Campbell's early history little that is definite is known. He is believed to have been born in Missouri, and as a lad to have been apprenticed to a blacksmith. It is known that later on he appeared in New York and worked as a machinist in the printing-press manufactory of A. B. Taylor. It was while he was employed there that Moses Beach of the *Sun* offered a prize for a successful cylinder press adapted for use by small newspapers. It was this offer that led Campbell to invent and to successfully develop his Country Press, which has subsequently become famous, and of which there are nearly 5000 in use to-day.

PAGE DESIGNED BY WILL BRADLEY
FROM "THE CAMPBELL BOOK"

A History of New York

Book VI. Containing the second part of the reign of PETER THE HEADSTRONG, and his gallant achievements on the Delaware.

CHAPTER I. In which is exhibited a *warlike portrait* of the *great* PETER— and how *General Van Poffenburgh* distinguished himself at *Fort Casimir*

ITHERTO, most venerable and courteous reader, have I shown thee the administration of the valorous Stuyvesant, under the mild moonshine of peace, or rather the grim tranquillity of awful expectation; but now the war-drum rumbles from afar, the brazen trumpet brays its thrilling note, and the rude clash of hostile arms speaks fearful prophecies of coming troubles. The gallant warrior starts from soft repose, from golden visions, and voluptuous ease; where, in the dulcet, "piping time of peace," he sought sweet solace after all his toils. No more in beauty's syren lap reclined, he weaves fair garlands for his lady's brows; no more entwines with flowers his shining sword, nor through the livelong lazy summer's day chants forth his lovesick soul in madrigals. To manhood roused, he spurns the amorous flute; doffs from his brawny back the robe of peace, and clothes his pampered limbs in panoply of steel. O'er his dark brow, where late the myrtle waved, where wanton roses breathed enervate love, he rears the beaming casque and nodding plume; grasps the bright shield and shakes the ponderous lance; or mounts with eager pride his fiery steed, and burns for deeds of glorious chivalry!

But soft, worthy reader! I would not have you imagine, that any *preux chevalier*, thus hideously begirt with iron, existed in the city of New-Amsterdam. This is but a lofty and gigantic mode in which heroic writers always talk of war, thereby to give it a noble and imposing aspect; equipping our warriors with bucklers, helms, and lances, and such like outlandish and obsolete weapons, the like of which perchance they had never seen or heard of; in the same manner that a cunning

FRONTISPIECE AND TITLE-PAGE DESIGNED BY BRUCE ROGERS FROM "ESSAYS OF MONTAIGNE" (HOUGHTON, MIFFLIN AND CO.)

280

BOOKE I.

THE AUTHOR TO THE READER.

READER, loe here a well-meaning Booke. It doth at the first entrance forewarne thee, that, in contriving the same, I have proposed unto my selfe no other than a familiar and private end; I have no respect or consideration at all, either to thy service, or to my glory; my forces are not capable of any such desseigne. I have vowed the same to the particular commodity of my kinsfolks and friends: to the end that, losing me (which they are likely to doe ere long), they may therein find some lineaments of my conditions and humours, and by that meanes reserve more whole, and more lively foster the knowledge and acquaintance they have had of me. Had my intention beene to forestall and purchase the worlds opinion and favour, I would surely have adorned my selfe more quaintly, or kept a more grave and solemne march.[1] I desire therein to be delineated in mine owne genuine, simple, and ordinarie fashion, without contention, art, or study; for it is my selfe I pourtray. My imperfections shall therein be read to the life, and my naturall forme discerned, so farre-forth as publike reverence hath permitted me. For if my fortune had beene to have lived among those nations, which yet are said to live under the sweet libertie of Natures first and uncorrupted lawes, I assure thee, I would most willingly have pourtrayed my selfe fully and naked. Thus, gentle Reader, my selfe am the groundworke of my booke: it is then no reason thou shouldest employ thy time about so frivolous and vaine a Subject.[2] Therefore farewell.

From MONTAIGNE, the first of March. 1580.

THE FIRST CHAPTER.

By divers meanes men come unto a like end.

HE most usuall way to appease those minds we have offended (when revenge lies in their hands, and that we stand at their mercy) is, by submission to move them to commiseration and pitty. Nevertheless, courage, constancie, and resolution (meanes altogether opposite) have sometimes wrought the same effect. Edward the black Prince of Wales (who so long governed our Country of Guienne, a man whose conditions and fortune were accompanied with many notable parts of worth and magnanimitie) having beene grievously offended by the Limosins, though he by maine force tooke and entred their Citie, could by no meanes be appeased, nor by the waile-full out-cries of all sorts of people (as of men, women, and children) be moved to any pitty, they prostrating themselves to the common slaughter, crying for mercy, and humbly submitting themselves at his feet, untill such time as in triumphant manner passing thorow their Citie, he perceived three French Gentlemen,' who alone, with an incredible and undaunted boldnesse, gainstood the enraged violence, and made head against the furie of his victorious armie. The consideration and respect of so notable a vertue did first abate the dint of his wrath, and from those three began to relent, and shew mercy to all the other inhabitants of the said towne. Scanderbeg, Prince of Epirus,[2] following one of his souldiers, with purpose to kill him, who, by all means of humilitie and submisse entreatie, had first assaied to pacifie him, in such an unavoidable extremitie, resolved at last resolutely to encounter him with his sword in his hand. This resolution did immediately stay his Captains fury, who, seeing him undertake so honourable an attempt, not only forgave, but received him into grace and favour. This example may haply, of such as have not knowne the prodigious force and matchlesse valour of the said Prince, admit

OPENING PAGES PRINTED IN THE "MONTAIGNE" TYPE DESIGNED BY BRUCE ROGERS FROM "ESSAYS OF MONTAIGNE" (HOUGHTON, MIFFLIN AND CO.)

INITIAL LETTERS DESIGNED BY BRUCE ROGERS. FROM
"ESSAYS OF MONTAIGNE" (HOUGHTON, MIFFLIN AND CO.)

282

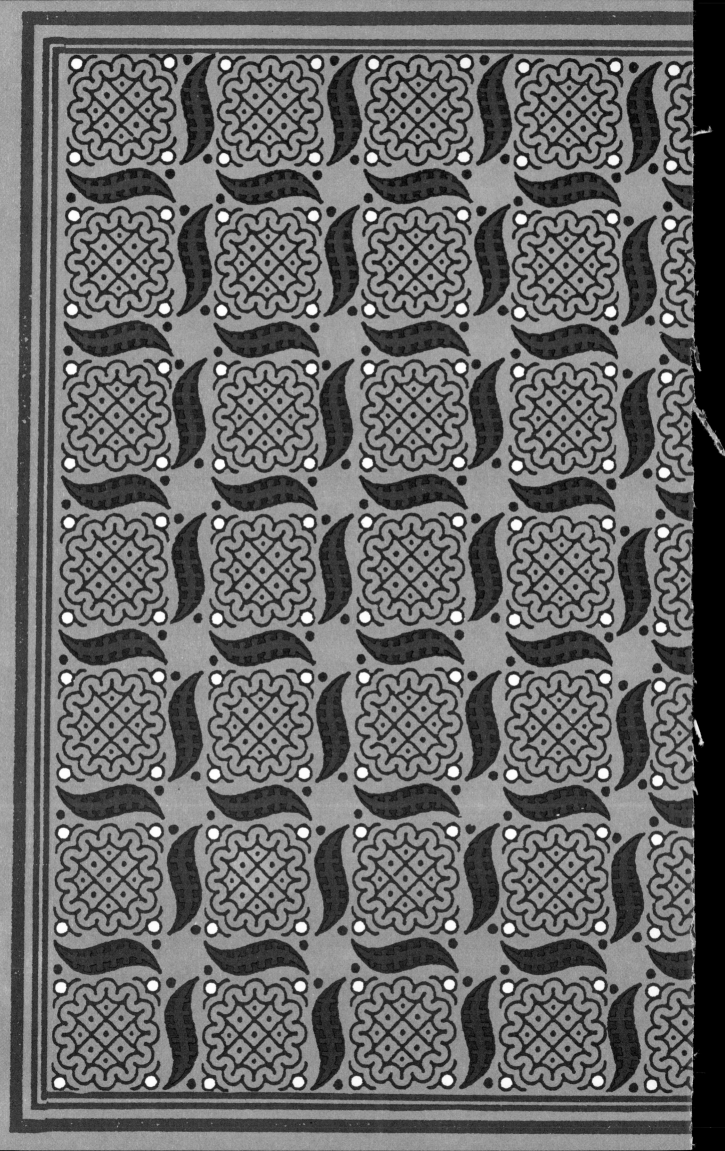